Born Into Trafficking Rescued A Virgin

A Testimony of Human Trafficking
and God's Divine Intervention
Abigail Piper Jordan

Revival Fire Press

Illustrations by Abigail Jordan

Cover design by 99designs

Published by Revival Fire Press

First Edition | 2025

Paperback ISBN: 979-8-9993723-9-0
eBook ISBN: 979-8-9993723-0-7

Printed in the United States of America

Trigger Warning & Content Note

This book includes real-life accounts of trauma, abuse, human trafficking, and spiritual experiences. While the author shares her story from a place of healing and hope, some readers may find portions of the content emotionally intense or triggering.
Please read with care and seek support from a trusted counselor, support group, or faith leader if needed.

Dedication

This book is dedicated to those who are healing—and to the helpers who walk alongside the ones held captive by human trafficking. I want to acknowledge my adopted family, whose faithful love has been a constant reflection of God's strength. And to my dear husband—thank you for standing by my side as I wrote this book.

Contents

Part 1
The Beginnings

Revival Fire Press

Introduction

This book was not easy to write.

It holds memories I once believed would remain buried forever—wounds too deep, moments too dark, and truths too painful to face. But as I've learned through years of healing, counseling, and walking with others, what stays hidden can continue to control us. And what is brought into the light can finally begin to heal.

I wrote Born into Trafficking, Rescued a Virgin because my story is not just mine—it's the story of countless others who have been silenced by trauma, shaped by survival, and left wondering if hope still exists. For years, I have shared my testimony through public speaking, counseling, and ministry. But this book offers something deeper: unfiltered access to the journey I lived—including human trafficking, satanic ritual abuse, illegal experimentation, deep psychological trauma, and the presence of God who never let go.

Whether you are a survivor, a ministry leader, a counselor, or someone trying to understand how trauma affects the body, mind, and spirit—I pray this book gives you more than information. I pray it offers revelation, compassion, and a glimpse of the God who still sets captives free.

Revival, to me, was never just an emotional experience—it was a divine rescue. Every moment in God's presence became a lifeline. I could feel Him breathing life into places I thought were dead. Revival was the hand of God reaching down from heaven, healing me, restoring me, and reminding me that he had spoken purpose over my life long before I understood it.

Revival became the evidence that God had never stopped pursuing me. And Jesus—Jesus is the key to revival. That is what this book is about.

At just five years old, I heard the Lord say, "Stand up in My name no matter what—and one day you will understand."

That day is today.

—Abigail Jordan

Chapter 1
What is Human Trafficking?

Human trafficking is a multifaceted issue around the world that involves the exploitation of children, women, and men for financial or personal gain. At its core, human trafficking consists of the trade of people against their will, forcing them into situations of servitude such as sexual exploitation, forced labor, and other forms of slavery.

Trafficking is a complex and widespread criminal activity with various forms of exploitation. While sex trafficking and labor trafficking are the primary categories recognized under the Trafficking Victims Protection Act (TVPA), human trafficking also includes several other forms, each marked by unique patterns of control and abuse.[1].

My Personal Experience

Throughout my life, I have witnessed and endured many forms of trafficking firsthand. Born into a trafficking situation, I experienced exploitation in ways that I will share throughout this book. My goal is to help others understand what this looks like, especially when it begins in childhood. I want to shed light on some of the specific trafficking I faced.

Sex and Child Trafficking

People who are coerced or forced into commercial sexual acts suffer exploitation through prostitution and pornography, either under the age of 18 or adult age. By law, anyone under 18 involved in sex work is considered a trafficking victim—even if they appeared to agree. Children face additional exploitation through other forced illegal acts such as drug dealing, theft, or smuggling, for the purpose of servitude.

Children who are kidnapped or manipulated lack autonomy or the means to seek help, frequently forced into domestic servitude, [2]where isolation intensifies their vulnerability. This isolation often includes being cut off from school, friends, or safe adults—making it easier for traffickers to stay in control.

Commercial Sexual Exploitation

Any child under 18 involved in commercial sex is legally considered a trafficking victim, regardless of force, fraud, or coercion. Adults who are coerced into prostitution or pornography are also victims of sex trafficking. Children trafficked not just for sex but also for drug trafficking, theft, or other illicit activities are still under the umbrella of trafficking, as they are exploited for someone else's gain. In every case, trafficking strips a person of choice, freedom, and safety. It turns a human being into a commodity—and that's what makes it so damaging.

Illegal Human Experimentation

If children (or anyone) are forced to participate in experiments subjected to medical, military, or scientific experiments without consent, especially under coercion or threat, it is considered forced labor because they are compelled to "work" (participate in experiments) against their will. The coercion often involves brutal indoctrination, physical violence, and deception[3].

In my case, I was sold into such situations by my own parents. Modern-day human trafficking is illegal under U.S. and international law, involving the use of force, fraud, or coercion to exploit victims for commercial sex, labor, or other services. Victims often face blackmail and severe coercion, instilling pervasive fear through threats of violence against themselves and loved ones, severely limiting their ability to escape.[4]

A basic principle that drives traffickers is that whatever can be commodified and sold for money will be. It is plain evil! It does not care that you are human.

Traffickers' goal is to make the most profit from an individual sold. From my own life experiences being born into trafficking, it extends beyond physical, encompassing psychological manipulation and coercion.

Human trafficking targets people and communities regardless of their environment, government, religion, or economic status. It's indiscriminate; it doesn't matter where you're from; it will invade your life given the chance. Its motivation is greed; it seeks to exploit, deceive, and control individuals.

It is a distressing reality found in many cities and towns across the United States, including local communities, schools, and even targeted churches. Traffickers meticulously groom entire communities, similar to how they groom individual victims, often appearing as wolves in sheep's clothing.

Mental Health and Human Trafficking

One of the greatest challenges in addressing human trafficking is its deceptive nature. Trafficking often hides in plain sight, making it difficult for even well-intentioned individuals to recognize. This invisibility is compounded by the deep psychological harm inflicted on survivors, which can mask or complicate the signs of abuse.

The trauma experienced during trafficking frequently leads to serious mental health consequences. Many survivors develop symptoms of post-traumatic stress disorder (PTSD), including nightmares, flashbacks, and intense emotional distress. [5]Anxiety, depression, and suicidal thoughts are also common.

Dissociation is another common response—survivors may feel disconnected from their bodies, emotions, or surroundings. This mental distancing often develops as a survival mechanism in the face of over-whelming abuse.

Many survivors fluctuate between hyperarousal, marked by irritability and heightened vigilance, and hypoarousal, where numbness or emotional shut-down takes over. [6]These patterns often show up as fight, flight, or freeze responses—instinctive survival reactions shaped by prolonged trauma.[7]

Trauma to Triumph: My Journey Through Dissociation

My life began in trafficking, and I will share my ex-periences with trauma, particularly its impact on me through dissociation. Disconnecting from reality of-ten serves as a coping mechanism for overwhelming stress and is commonly associated with a trauma re-sponse.

According to world-renowned psychiatrist Bessel van der Kolk, dissociation[8] is a natural defense mech-anism during trauma, allowing the brain to separate from unbearable emotional or physical experiences. This disconnection may be temporary, but for many survivors, it becomes a conditioned response that continues long after the trauma ends. [9]

While helpful at the moment, dissociation can evolve into a maladaptive coping strategy that impairs daily functioning over time. Dissociation helped me survive abuse but left me more vulnerable to even further exploitation. As you hear my story, you will sense the weight of the darkest moments in my life. Yet, these moments are contrasted by the hope and deliverance I found in God.

A Call to Action for the Church

As a Christian, you have the power to combat the darkness of human trafficking. My story is a testament to God's intervention, rescue, and healing as you learn of God bringing me to revival atmospheres. I believe the church is a key to the fight against human trafficking because it represents God's love, grace, and redemption.

In order to effectively combat human trafficking, the church needs revival—an awakening that opens our eyes to see the harsh realities and hidden evil around us. Right now, many are spiritually asleep, unaware or indifferent to the suffering happening in our own communities.

Revival is essential because it stirs our hearts, awakens our spirits, and gives us God's perspective on injustice. Revival breaks through complacency and calls us to repentance, allowing the Holy Spirit to purify our hearts, and we are bolden to take action. When revival touches the church, we begin to see clearly—no longer blind to the suffering and injustice around us.

Our hearts break for what breaks God's heart, and we are moved to action.

God's promises gives us hope.

> "If my people, who are called by my name, will humble themselves and pray and seek my face and turn from their wicked ways, then I will hear from heaven, and I will forgive their sin and will heal their land."(2 Chronicles 7:14 NIV)

Human trafficking is not only a physical and psychological crime, but also a spiritual battle.

> Ephesians 6:12 reminds us, "For our struggle is not against flesh and blood, but against the rulers, against the authorities, against the powers of this dark world and against the spiritual forces of evil in the heavenly realms."(NIV)

To stand against trafficking, we must not only fight physically through awareness and intervention but also spiritually through prayer, fasting, and intercession. Prayer and repentance are the church's strongest weapons.

My goal is to share my testimony to equip churches for the coming revival that will sweep through churches in America. When God moves upon the church, a harvest of souls and those who once were held captive by human trafficking will have a safe place to heal. There is healing in God's manifest presence.

The church can make a difference by:

Educating congregations about human trafficking.

Partnering with local organizations to offer shelter and support.

Training leaders to recognize the signs of trafficking and respond appropriately.

Praying intentionally for victims and survivors.

As a survivor, I hope this book will help you grasp a better understanding of the hidden horrors of human trafficking, a reality that I know all too well. I lived most of my entire life in the deep pits of human trafficking and was silenced, but now I speak. My story of surviving human trafficking will help you understand and fight this horrific crime.

---

1. **Source:** U.S. Department of State. Trafficking in Persons Report, 2023. https://www.state.gov/reports/2023-trafficking-in-persons-report/

2. **Source:** Polaris. (2023). Sex trafficking statistics. Polaris Project. https://polarisproject.org/human-trafficking/. According to Polaris, traffickers commonly exploit children's dependence and social isolation, making them especially vulnerable to being trapped in domestic labor or hidden servitude, with minimal opportunities to escape or seek protection.

3. **Source:**Toney-Butler, T. J., Ladd, M., & Mittel, O. (2023). Human trafficking. StatPearls Publishing. https://www.ncbi.nlm.nih.gov/books/NBK430910/. StatPearls outlines that forced labor can include coercive participation in labor-like activities, including experimentation, when victims are threatened, deceived, or violently compelled—particularly in vulnerable populations.

4. **Source:** U.S. Department of Justice. (n.d.). What is human trafficking? https://www.justice.gov/humantrafficking. The DOJ defines human trafficking as a crime involving the exploitation of individuals through force, fraud, or coercion. It also notes that traffickers often use threats, blackmail, and emotional manipulation to maintain control over victims and prevent escape.

5. American Psychiatric Association. (2013). Diagnostic and statistical manual of mental disorders (5th ed.). Arlington, VA: American Psychiatric Publishing.

6. American Psychiatric Association. (2013). Diagnostic and statistical manual of mental disorders (5th ed.). Arlington, VA: American Psychiatric Publishing. The DSM-5 outlines dissociation and arousal dysregulation—including hyper- and hypoarousal—as hallmark responses in trauma-related disorders such as PTSD and dissociative disorders.

7. **Source:** Van der Kolk, B. A. (2014). The body keeps the score: Brain, mind, and body in the healing of trauma. New York: Viking. Van der Kolk explains that traumatic experiences reorganize the brain's perception of threat and safety, often resulting in survival-driven responses such as fight, flight, freeze, or collapse.

8. **Source:** Van der Kolk, B. A. (2014). The body keeps the score: Brain, mind, and body in the healing of trauma.

9. **Source:** Van der Kolk, B. A. (2014). The body keeps
the score: Brain, mind, and body in the healing of
trauma. New York: Viking. Van der Kolk explains
that dissociation is the brain's way of surviving
overwhelming stress, but over time, this protective strategy can become habitual and interfere
with daily functioning and identity integration.

Chapter 2
Introduction From Abigail

Hi, my name is Abigail, but I was originally named Tabitha at birth. I have a twin sister named Jennifer. I share this with you at the beginning of my story so that you can clearly understand the importance of the name change and its significance.

I plan to present my life story in a timeline format, which will help you follow along as I recount the events that have shaped who I am today. To protect the privacy of those involved, I will use different names for other people spoken of in this book.

While I don't remember every little detail, I will share the most accurate recollections of the significant moments. In this book, I will narrate my entire life story, illustrating how I transformed into the person I am today.

Background Information

My twin and I were born in Dallas, Texas, in 1976. My father, mother, and paternal grandparents were deeply involved in satanic occult practices, human trafficking, sex trafficking, gun and drug smuggling with gangs, military experiments, medical experiments, baby parts harvesting, and other forms of slavery across generations.

I had two older brothers, Michael and Phil, and an older sister, Anna, who had faced their challenges to survive. A few years later, after my twin sister Gena and I were born, I gained two half-brothers, Eron and Taylor.

As a child, we moved a lot between Texas and Tennessee. Finally, we settled in Duncanville, Texas, but still changed homes often. My early years, before turning five, were a time of great confusion and complexity. During these first five years of life, the abuse that I had endured from the human trafficking experiments, sex trafficking, and satanic occult abuse led me into a continuous reactive state of mind to dissociation due to repeated exposure to trafficking.

You might wonder why I didn't tell anyone about the abuse and trafficking. Was there no one safe I could trust? The idea of confiding in an adult brought a wave of fear I couldn't put into words. Sadly, many children suffer in silence. That silence is not weakness—it's a survival response to a deeply terrifying reality.

Talking about sex can often feel shameful, and shame played a crucial role in keeping me silent. As my perpetrators frequently reminded me, if you tell anyone, others will be hurt, and it will be your fault;

you actually enjoyed it, you chose to participate, and you are bad.

As I got older, my behavior in middle school became more and more disruptive, but it wasn't just me being rebellious. It was my way of crying out for help, trying to show people that something was terribly wrong. I didn't know how to put what I was going through into words, and I didn't trust any adults.

I was convinced that even if I did speak up to someone I trusted, corrupt government officials involved in trafficking would find out and make things even worse, as I was often reminded of the consequences if I told. This was my reality as a child—living with the fear that the adults around me, who were part of the trafficking, would silence me if I tried to tell the truth. Early on, I learned that trust was dangerous and that my voice was something to be kept hidden. I became conditioned to believe that no one could protect me, and the world around me only confirmed that fear.

Fear kept me silent, as speaking out felt like it would endanger my family and loved ones. Escape seemed impossible. Watching my abusers punish and humiliate others was a deliberate way to keep me quiet. This was my reality.

Life as a Baby

As a baby, I had an innate desire to be held and to connect with others, which is a natural desire in all of us. One vivid memory I have from my infancy is the feeling of intense loneliness in my crib, coupled with an overwhelming desire to see another person. This desire manifested itself in my desperate cries.

Little did I know that the emotional neglect and psychological abuse I experienced daily from my parents would not only deprive me of love and affection but also inflict the opposite, leaving me feeling deeply hurt and abandoned. I realized this marked the beginning of my life, a life filled with experiences contrary to the original design God had destined me for. I did not experience love or nurturance from my parents in my childhood; my beginning was pure hell as my life began with being sold into sex trafficking, satanic ritual abuse, and illegal human experiments.

Erik Erikson, a well-known ego psychologist recognized for his theories on the eight stages of psychosocial development, explains that the first stage, trust versus mistrust, occurs during infancy and focuses on the infant's need for consistent and reliable care to develop a sense of security. [1] That deep longing yearning in my childhood to be loved is only seen through mistrust.

This compelled me, even in my infancy, to develop self-preservation skills to survive the abuse. One thought I have pondered is this: if I desire self-preservation, then God must have purposed me to be here on this earth for a reason. My answer was found not in the voices of others, but in the words God had written over me from the beginning. In a season when I felt unworthy, fragmented, and invisible, this passage from Psalm 139 reminded me that I had always been seen, known, and deeply loved.

> For you created my inmost being; you knit me together in my mother's womb. I praise you because I am fearfully and wonderfully made; your works are wonderful, I know that full well. My frame was not hidden from you when I was made in the secret place, when I was woven together in the depths of the earth.Your eyes saw my unformed body; all the days ordained for me were written in your book before one of them came to be. How precious to me are your thoughts, God! How vast is the sum of them! Were I to count them, they would outnumber the grains of sand—when I awake, I am still with you.(Psalm 139:13–18, NIV) [2]

This scripture reaffirmed that God had a purpose for me. He created every part of me—my creativity, artistry,intelligence, compassion, sensitivity, discernment, and stubbornness.

My twin and I, though in some ways, had distinct personalities. I was highly sensitive, picking up on others' emotions and body language, but I was also needy and dependent. In contrast, my twin was more independent and had a fiery, engaging personality.

Childhood experiences shape how we see ourselves and others. While Psalm 139 reassured me of God's intentional design,my parents' unhealthy affection instilled a deep mistrust of adults. Paradoxically, this mistrust became my shield, enabling me to survive unimaginable pain. Even without nurturing care, God's hand equipped me with resilience, affirming that my survival had a purpose.

---

1. **Source:** Erikson, E. H. (1963). Childhood and society (2nd ed.). New York: W. W. Norton & Company.

2. **Source:** Scripture quotation taken from the Holy Bible, New International Version®. Copyright © 1973, 1978, 1984, 2011 by Biblica, Inc.® Used by permission. All rights reserved worldwide.

Chapter 3

Networking: Satanism & Human Trafficking

N etworking played a significant role in both human trafficking and the operations of the Satanic occult, enabling perpetrators to collaborate, conceal
crimes, and expand their reach across regions and
institutions.

During my childhood, I was immersed in a world
of Satanic rituals and various cult beliefs, including
freemasonry, anarchy, agnosticism, and diverse poly-
theistic religions.

Each of these belief systems emphasized the pursuit
of power and status, often at the expense of moral values, resulting in a culture that embraced wickedness
and demonstrated little compassion for others.

These networks often formed alliances that re-
volved around human trafficking and the New World
Order, with members bound by their shared dedica-
tion to these dark practices.

Generational Cycle of the Occult

My family's Satanism was rooted in the belief that God had abandoned humanity while Satan offered the freedom to indulge selfish desires. This ideology fueled my father's deep involvement in the occult and human trafficking, continuing a generational cycle that began with my paternal grandparents.

My mother's role in these practices is less clear and remains unknown, though I suspect it was influenced by the violence and threats she endured, as I witnessed during my childhood.

Instinctive Morality: A Toddler's Perspective

In my upbringing within the satanic cult, Bible scripture was often twisted to justify Satanism or mock Christianity. I remember being around two years old, and my parents claimed our house was haunted by spirits, telling stories of ghosts in the attic and basement and of moving doors.

As a child, I began to reason with the thought of the reality of fear and the devil; there must also be a good God who wanted us to feel happy and safe.

In the satanic cult and my upbringing, they twisted Bible scripture to justify Satanism and mock Christianity, which made me question what is true. I couldn't comprehend my father's hatred and participation in

Satanic practices, but it made me realize that my mistrust of my parents and the surrounding adults in my life was justified.

My young 2-year-old self could not believe what I was experiencing was a good thing. Despite my lack of analytic skills as a child, I instinctively knew right from wrong, a clear, innate sense of morality shaped by my belief in a good God and a bad devil.

A Defining Memory: God is Good, and the Devil is Bad

One particular moment stands out in my memory—a moment when I was two years old moment that solidified my belief that God is good and the devil is bad. One afternoon, my father called out to me and had me walk with him to our backyard, where we had a old shed next to our small cornfield and garden bordering our home in Tennessee. My father and I entered the shed, which was filled with tools and a table.

He slowly removed each piece of my clothing before laying me on the table, securing my hands and feet, and finally positioning me on my back with my face looking towards the ceiling of the shed.

Scared and unsure of what might happen, I remained still. I was used to my father witnessing me naked and sexually abusing me. I watched my father as he held in his hands a huge knife, I thought he was going to kill me!

I was terrified.

At that moment, I mustered up the courage to say aloud to him, " "God is good and the devil is bad".

When I recall this memory, I remember the heavy weight of my words, the desperate hope in my voice as I tried to convince my father of the truth and save myself. The look on his face when I stated, "God is good, and the devil is bad," is forever imprinted in my mind; his face looked perplexed that I said that.

My father immediately left me alone in the shed and returned with one of our pet rabbits. He then began to sacrifice the rabbit on top of me and speak incomprehensible words I could not make sense of. He spread the blood of the rabbit all over my little body. Then he hung the rabbit's lifeless body overtop of me, and its blood drained on top of me.

That day, my stated words declaring, "God is good, and the devil is bad," became my foundational truth and reality.

> In Matthew 17:20 states, "For truly, I say to you, if you have faith like a grain of mustard seed, you will say to this mountain, 'Move from here to there,' and it will move, and nothing will be impossible for you." (NIV)

What began as fear and a trembling voice, I found the courage to declare a foundational truth despite potential consequences from my father. That moment of fragile faith, as small as a mustard seed, marked the beginning of my journey.

Chapter 4
Unethical Human Experimentation

Human traffickers exploit everything they can to make money, including a person's body, mind, identity, and sense of self. The constant exposure to trauma became too much for me to bear, and I began to dissociate as a way to survive.

Dissociation is a common trauma response that helps protect the mind by disconnecting from present reality. For me, it became a way to block out the abuse and endure overwhelming pain.

Tragically, my parents took advantage of this natural defense mechanism. They used my dissociative states to involve me in illegal scientific experiments designed to instill fear and manipulate my behavior—what I refer to as mind programming. Over time, dissociation became a survival tool that split and fragmented my identity. It allowed me to emotionally detach and shield myself from the fear, rejection, and humiliation I faced.

To preserve my core self from the relentless abuse and manipulation—by both my parents and the men I call observatory men—I dissociated even further. This fragmentation became my way to survive. Though horrifying to acknowledge, research and survivor accounts confirm that severe childhood trauma can lead to identity fragmentation as a form of psychological protection. [1]

Mind Programming

In the course of these illegal human experiments, I experienced what I call mind programming. This involved deliberate attempts by my abusers to manipulate my mind by exploiting the dissociative states caused by trauma. In simple terms, this meant intentionally forcing different parts of my identity to surface, shaping them into specific roles, behaviors, or responses.

Some of these identities were created through the coercion of my abusers. Others were influenced by my parents. Still others arose from within me—internal defenses formed in my effort to survive what felt unendurable. The result was a fragmented inner world, one that responded to domination, fear, and control by breaking apart in order to stay alive. [23]

Sedation and Drug Use

My traffickers didn't just manipulate my mind; they also controlled me with sedatives and forced drug use throughout my trafficking experience. When I was a child, the stress of traumatic situations sometimes pushed my body into shock. To manage this, they would put me into ice baths or massage me out of shock.

Sedatives were used frequently, not just to control me, but to keep me alive during these moments. One of my earliest memories of sedation was being given alcohol in my baby bottle as an infant.

Later, during my preteen and teenage years, I believe I was injected with heroin as a way to keep me subdued. Forced drugging was a constant method of control, just as powerful as the manipulation of my dissociation.

Illegal Human Experimentation

As you have learned of the exploitation and control of traffickers, This chapter looks at human trafficking within the context of illegal human experimentation driven by unknown scientific motives.

In my experience, these experiments were brutal and invasive, involving scientific research without consent, constant monitoring, and observation. Many people may not realize that this kind of trafficking exists, as it is rarely talked about compared to other forms. Tragically, it often involves parents selling their children into these illegal experiments. This kind of trafficking uses psychological abuse, manipulation, deception, and coercion to force victims into abusive situations, leaving lasting trauma and control.

This chapter shares my early memories, not just of sex trafficking, but of being initiated into illegal scientific experimental trafficking from a very young age. These experiences are just the beginning, and later chapters will continue to explore the impact and details of this hidden and horrifying reality.

Pooh and Tiger: Age 2

Through dissociation, I developed identity disturbances and adopted alter personalities linked to trauma from human trafficking, guided by both my perpetrator and me. Pooh was the first nickname I received from my father, and he used to call my twin Tiger, trying to compare our personalities and temperaments with the cartoon characters from the cartoon show, "Winnie the Pooh."

My father loved to tell the story of how I got the nickname Pooh, relating it to my intense emotional sensitivity, which became a way of entertainment for my father whenever I was an infant. In my father's memory, he often recounts the tale of my siblings huddled together on his bed as he lifted me high in the air, stretching his arms wide as I gazed up at him.

Then, his voice shifted from excitement to a gentle, soft tone as he said,

"Now, Pooh. Now, Pooh."

Afterward, he explained,

"You would become tearful, your lips would begin to shiver, and then you would start to cry."

My emotional sensitivity only served to entertain my father, whose harsh laughter filled the air.

The College Experiment Begins Ages 3–4

Looking back, I believe I was around three years old when my father began to see my emotional sensitivity as a resourceful way to make money—using both my twin and me for profit.

He brought us to a small local college in Tennessee, where he claimed we were part of an observatory experiment. I remember holding his hand as we walked through a crowd of college students. We returned to that place multiple times.

Each visit, my twin and I were watched by two men in white coats who met with us in one of the college rooms. As a child, I didn't know what to call them—I had no words for who they were or what they were doing. But as I write this now, I call them the observatory men. It's the only name that seems to fit. I can only assume they were scientists or researchers of some kind.

We were placed in separate, transparent square containers—deep and inescapable. Once inside, white cords were connected to various parts of our upper bodies.

While observing our reactions, the observatory men would exaggerate different facial expressions marked with emotion. They wrote in charts as if our pain were data to them .

The most traumatic memory I have of those sessions was one of the observatory men screaming in my face, making loud, sudden noises all around me.

Of course, I cried. I was scared. I was petrified

Even my father was not in the room, and we were left with these two men, which made me feel even less secure and safe. At least I knew my father's face and knew I belonged to him.

My father's soft "Now Pooh, Now Pooh" was what I was accustomed to, but the erratic behavior of the two men in white coats from the college shattered my sense of security.

The continuous attempts to provoke my twin and I created a confusing and unsettling atmosphere. After the college scientists had completed their unethical illegal studies, my father wasted no time. After learning more about my temperament, he had me participate in several future experiments as a child alone, without my twin.

The Chimpanzee Experiment Age 4

I was in a cage in Tennessee, out in the mountains, when the same two observatory men in white coats from the college came again. This time, they were observing my behavior and interactions with a chimpanzee.

I didn't want to leave the cage. I was scared. I didn't know what to do. I noticed the scientists weren't afraid of the chimpanzee—one of them even walked up to my cage and unlatched the door.

Instinctively, I backed away into the corner, curling into a fetal position. I kept my eyes on the chimpanzee, trying to keep a distance between us. The chimpanzee didn't approach right away. I don't remember exactly what he did at first.

I wish I could understand the purpose behind this experiment—but how could I? I was a child, already trafficked and traumatized, and this was just one more form of exploitation. I was brought back to this cage multiple times, and each time, they seemed to be testing whether I would interact with the chimpan zee.Eventually; they tried to force it. I remember one of the men lifting part of the cage, trying to make me slide or fall out. My body curled up again. I screamed in fear, terrified the chimpanzee would attack me. My memory blurs after that.

But what I wonder now is—how did the chimpanzee feel? He, too, was forced into this unnatural situation, far from his environment. Maybe he was scared, too. Maybe we were both victims—two beings forced into a shared trauma for someone else's idea of "research."

Whatever they were trying to prove, I know this: no valid experiment is based on coercion, fear, and abuse. What they did to me—and possibly to him—was not science. It was cruelty.

Mountain Experiment: Tag Age 4

Soon after the chimpanzee experiment, my father involved me in another experiment. I recall it being close to dark at night, and the cool temperature in the Tennessee mountains reminded me of this memory. My father referred to me by the nickname "Tag" as he walked with me a long way through the mountains. At home, he had given me that name after watching me one day, playing the game outside with my siblings and a few neighbors in our front yard.

As we stopped walking, it appeared that the same two observatory men in the white coats from the community college were awaiting us. My father told me, "Wait right here." Then he went to talk with those two men from a distance.

I played along, pretending to be ignorant, even though my stomach turned. Little did I know, my father and the two men would suddenly run off together, leaving me alone. I remembered how these men had acted at the community college—their behavior was unpredictable—so I wasn't sure if I was being watched or if something unexpected was about to happen.

I stayed on alert, paying close attention to every sound. I wanted to keep my feelings hidden, but the pressure inside me was too much, and I began to cry. After being left alone, the trees seemed much taller, and every sound—whether a bird or a squirrel—grew louder in my ears.

I thought about how those observatory men might be watching me from a distance, and somehow, that thought brought a strange kind of comfort. It made me feel like I wasn't completely alone.

My past experiences of being left alone with those two men created a strong association in my mind: whenever the two men were present, I believed my father would disappear. I was trying to make sense of it all.

To survive that night, I clung to any optimistic thought that could offer even a tiny measure of comfort, using these hopeful ideas as my only survival technique. My quiet-natured personality worked very hard to stay calm, but I was merely trembling on the inside, often bursting into tears.

As it grew later into the night, I became more scared. I climbed a small area of a tree, thinking maybe I would be safer there, especially as the animal noises grew louder in the dark.

I never saw those observatory men again that night. Throughout the night, I cried out of desperate despair—because I was all alone and scared to be alone. I felt cold and thirsty. My feet hurt from trying to climb the trees.

As the sun rose early that morning, my father and mother appeared, along with my twin sister, older sister, and the two observatory men.

My emotions were mixed. I felt a sigh of relief, and some of the feelings of abandonment began to fade—but there was also lingering uncertainty. What happened next was confusing and psychologically abusive.

The Mock Funeral

As my father approached me, he took me closer to the spot where he had originally talked with the observatory men the night before. This place in the mountains was not just a vacant spot. It was significant. It was near a big black box container, and next to that container was a hidden underground door.

I watched my father open it. You could tell this door had been camouflaged before, covered with leaves and the mountain's natural surroundings to keep it hidden. I watched him unlatch it—and I heard voices down in the hidden area below.

Then my father told me that I had died and that they had to bury me in the ground. Another word for it: a mock funeral. He put me into the big black box container, which was then placed into the underground hole.

The mock funeral was a psychological tactic used by my father and the others to instill fear and control over me. I was placed in pitch darkness.

I remember panicking:

I am not dead! I am not dead! Please help!

I cried. I begged.

I lay there—confused, scared. I could feel every part of my body screaming that I was alive.

I cried out to God.

I remember the mass confusion: If I was dead, how come nothing was changing?

Tag Experiments Continued

The "Tag" experiments continued based on that first mountain experiment. These events became part of more advanced tracking exercises, where I was followed through the woods or mountains. Later in childhood, as I got older, there were other times I found myself hiding from adult men—men who seemed to be part of both the trafficking ring and the satanic occult.

I often climbed into trees again, just like before. They repeated the pattern of forcing me to be barefoot. Sometimes I was given the choice to keep my blouse and pants, but not always.The experiments escalated. They turned into twisted games for the bad men—games that sometimes ended with me being shot with tranquilizer guns.

In conclusion, my early experience with the first mountain experiment, which began when I was just four years old, deeply affected my spirit. I felt isolated, unsafe, and overwhelmed by a deep sadness. But I know that what comes next—sharing my experiences with military human trafficking—will be even harder. It's a painful chapter. But it's one I must tell.

---

1. Sar, V. (2017). Parallel-distinct structures of internal world and external reality: Disavowing and re-claiming the self-identity in the aftermath of trauma-generated dissociation. Frontiers in Psychology, 8, 216. https://doi.org/10.3389/fpsyg.2017.00216

2. Ibid. Sar (2017) further describes how these dissociated self-states can be shaped by external abuse into specific behavioral roles—aligning with what survivors may refer to as "mind programming."

3. Dell, P. F., & O'Neil, J. A. (2009). Dissociation
   and the dissociative disorders: DSM-V and beyond. New York: Routledge. Dell and O'Neil also
   discuss how coercion and trauma can shape
   dissociated identities into role-bound behavioral
   states—similar to what survivors describe as
   "mind programming."

Chapter 5
Military Human Trafficking Begins

I want to take a moment to express my gratitude to the brave men and women who honorably serve our nation. What I'm about to share does not reflect the true heart or values of the United States Armed Forces—but rather the brokenness of individuals who abused power in ways never intended.

Human trafficking is a deep injustice, and it knows no boundaries—not even within the walls of our military. The truth must be told—not to tear down, but to bring light, healing, and justice.

What happened to me in military spaces was not about service or sacrifice—it was about control, exploitation, and the breaking down of a child's mind and body.

For years, I stayed silent, believing no one would believe me. But silence only protected those who hurt me. Speaking out is part of healing—and part of holding systems accountable.What came next was something I call the Hulk Experiments.

The Hulk Experiments Begin

After what I call the mountain experiment, my parents enrolled me in something I can only describe as the Hulk Experiments, which took place at an Air Force base in Tennessee. According to my parents, I had been given a "second chance at life" because I had survived being buried in the mountain. They said I had "passed the test" of escaping death, and now it was time to move on to the next phase—as if this was some kind of reward or achievement.

During the Hulk experiment, what shattered me the most was hearing constant reminders that I was not loved. My parents reminded me often that the only reason I was alive was to be part of these experiments.

I now understand that this was part of their plan to break down my identity and self-worth. As a child going through this, whenever I sought comfort from my parents during times of fear or distress, I was met with harsh words and rejection.

I often heard phrases like, "I hate you" or "We do not love you." Their lack of love and rejection left me feeling shameful towards myself—shattered, broken, lost, and full of despair.

It was not only my parents reminding me I was unloved, but also the other adults involved in the Hulk experiments—and the military personnel—would reinforce that I was unloved. Over time, the lack of love and emotional support pushed me to the point of being completely submissive to the adults around me.

The Spinning Chair

One of my first memories from the Air Force base is sitting in a white chair that spun around. It had a seatbelt that locked me in place. Nearby, there was a white box with electrode cords that were sometimes attached to my body. A military man oversaw the process, along with the two observatory men from the other experiments, whom I now believe were also military personnel.

If I didn't follow instructions, I would be punished. I received painful electric shocks while strapped in the chair. Sometimes, the chair would spin quickly, making me dizzy and disoriented.

The spinning and the shocks were terrifying.

Other occurrences that happened while I was strapped into the chair included being forced to watch my twin or my mother be abused in front of me, or witnessing animals killed. I was told that the reason these things were happening was because I wasn't following their instructions.

This filled me with anger and deep confusion. I began to internalize their words and believe that others were being hurt because of me. I developed intense self-hatred, believing it was my fault.

On top of that, they played tape recordings with loud, disturbing sounds and phrases meant to reprogram my mind and reinforce shame. These recordings were designed to convince me that I was the Hulk, that I was unlovable, and to instill feelings of shame, anger, and obedience. I began to lose my sense of self under this constant pressure, fear, and manipulation.

This drawing is taken while processing traumatic memories from the Air Force Base during a counseling session.

Becoming Hulk

I was four years old when the Hulk Experiments began. At that time, I had a stutter and lived in constant
fear. But by the time I turned five, the stutter was
gone—and I had become extremely obedient. I did
exactly what I was told, without question.

That was also when I first learned the word "report."
In the experiment, "report" meant I had to speak honestly about my feelings and experiences—but not as
myself. I had to talk from a different part of me, a
dissociative identity they called Hulk. I had to give up
control over my emotions and thoughts.

I later realized that the goal of these experiments
was to make me disconnect from myself—so I would
be easier to control and more likely to follow orders.
The word "report" became a strong trigger for me.

Whenever I had to report, I had to talk about
whether I had followed command instructions given
to me—whether it was about a past event, how I was
feeling, something from the experiments, or how I felt
inside—but always as Hulk, not as my true, real self.

Dissociation as Survival

The experiments went on for almost two years at
the Air Force base in Tennessee. During that time,
dissociation—mentally separating myself from what

was happening —became my way to survive the fear and pain. In the experiment environment, no one—including the military personnel and my own parents—called me by my real name. They only used the name Hulk. Over time, I began to believe that Hulk wasn't just a name—it was who I was.

The experiments were not only assigned at the Air Force base —they also continued at home. My mother would play the piano, often playing "The Lonely Man Theme" from the Incredible Hulk TV show. That song triggered something in me. I would feel small, scared, and submissive—especially around my parents. I remember once standing in the hallway while she played the piano. I froze beside her, full of fear. I wasn't angry like the Hulk on TV. I only got upset when I saw someone—or an animal—being hurt.

Because they kept calling me Hulk, I started to forget my real name. I would switch into different versions of the Hulk depending on what triggered me. Things like the color green, loud static noises, whistles, the Hulk theme song, piano music, or even seeing military uniforms could trigger me and connect back to those fears.

Eventually, I realized that dissociation was more than just something that happened to me—it was something I had learned to use to cope and survive. It helped me hide my true self and protect my emotions. The people in charge of the experiments wanted to turn me into a child soldier, but it didn't work. I used dissociation to stay safe, to stay hidden, and to eventually tell my story.

The Experiments Continue in Texas

The Hulk experiments continued as I moved to Texas around age 6. My understanding of this is limited. Even after moving from Tennessee, my father took me to other military bases in Texas, where I endured more torture and mind programming.

At a military base in Texas, I underwent waterboarding—a form of torture that involves covering the face with a rag while pouring water.

The tape recordings and electric shocks continued, and I felt my mind being controlled, instilling fear and obedience to their commands. Other forms of programming, I believe, included hypnosis and mind-altering drugs.

I was tortured, beaten down, and helpless. And for the mind programming—it worked, mostly. In a way, the Hulk became the alter ego that could reveal my deepest emotions and thoughts to the military, my father, or my mother, if I didn't express them myself as my core identity. The Hulk was programmed and created to report everything that was asked—remaining completely dedicated to my parents and the military.

I believe that part of the goal of the Hulk experiment was to have 100 percent control over me—and what I believe to be child soldiering.

What happened to me in the Hulk experiments is consistent with both coercion, involving the use of force or pressure to induce a particular behavior, and dissociation, a state of mental detachment from the torment and torture endured.

Later in life, the Hulk projects conditioned me to obey orders—to be in specific locations at precise times and dates, without hesitation. It felt as if I were a robot, simply carrying out instructions.

The Military and the Occult

These experiments continued until I was 17 years old. Even as a child and teenager, my father would intermittently take me back to the Air Force base in Tennessee. As I grew older, I noticed that some of the same military men who had been part of the Hulk experiments In Texas were also involved in the Satanic occult.

The Hulk experiment was partially successful because it relied on repeated exposure to constant abuse and fear. But the experiments failed in the long run—because I was able to continue dissociating as a form of self-preservation. It became the way I coped with the trauma, preserved my identity, and protected the person I truly was—the one I was created to be.

Their goal was to create a child soldier—but in the end, their success only proved one thing: they were bullies and cowards.

Chapter 6
The Beginning Stages: Sex Trafficking

The Grooming Stages

While being exposed to sex trafficking, I was reassured that this was an act of love, but during the Hulk experiment, persistent efforts were made to convince me that my parents did not love me. As a child, I wanted love from my parents, but I also felt that something was wrong. I felt shame and disgust, knowing that the sexual acts were wrong.

A part of me accepted my parents' version of love because I longed for love but this also made me believe I was a bad person, along with feeling a strong sense of shame that kept me silent and hidden from telling anyone of the sexual abuse.

I questioned myself, What if it's true?

What if I am as bad and unloving as the adults say?

It's still hard to even comprehend the emotional pain of knowing that someone who was supposed to protect and love me didn't. How could my father and mother sell their own children for sex?

My parents twisted love into abuse. They told me being sold to men was affection—that it was how I earned love or worth. I wanted love so badly, I believed the lie, even as it broke me.

First, my father was the first to groom and sexually molest me. It was the only time he would say, "I love you." Then, he would sell me for sex in our home in Tennessee to show his love.

My mother didn't protect me from sex trafficking or molestation by my father, causing me to suffer at the hands of my father. I realized she was submissive to my father, and she became my trafficker, too, although he was ultimately in charge of the sex trafficking. This was my reality; I was a victim of child sex trafficking.

Sex Trafficking Rule: No Name

When I was four years old, I played hide-and-seek outside at night with my siblings and other kids from the neighborhood near our house in Tennessee. It started as a fun game, but things quickly turned terrible. We were running around a small cornfield and hiding among the houses on our street.

As a car approached the stop sign next to our home, I saw my mother sitting in the passenger seat beside a man. When the man and my mother saw me, he rolled down his window. I was curious, so I asked him his name. He replied, "My name is 'no name'."

My mother then asked me to go inside the house with them. Once we were in her bedroom, the man started to rape me as she left me alone with him. Afterward, my mother scolded me and told me how bad I was for asking his name. From then on, my mother taught me to call men who did these things "No Name."

This was a new rule for me, and I did not understand why my mother became angry and spanked me. I was confused and deeply hurt by my mother.

When my father was in charge and sold me, I could always ask the men their names or had no restrictions. The little hope I had that my mother would rescue me from the life of abuse was gone after that night. That night, my mother became the main trafficker, which fractured any sense of safety and security, intensifying my feelings of vulnerability and isolation.

My Mother's Punishment

My father and mother twisted my understanding of love, turning abuse into something I was told to accept as affection. They made me believe that being sold to men was love—that this was how I earned closeness, attention, or worth. I wanted love so badly, I believed a lie—even while it was tearing me apart.

I always think of this memory—of my mother getting beat up—as being my fault, the result of me telling my father about my mother's new rule: "No Name."

One afternoon, my dad pulled into the driveway of our home in his pickup truck. My mother and I peeked out the window to watch him approach the front door. As he got out of his truck and began to walk toward the house, he was holding a bottle of Jack Daniel's. My mom looked nervous and said quietly, "He gets mean when he drinks."

I could see her fear, and it made me uneasy. Her fear intensified as he came up the steps, and I started to worry for her. Even after everything—despite the abuse I endured—I still loved my mom.

When my father opened the door, his boots hit the floor with a loud, heavy thud. I was terrified of what I was about to see.

Did I do something wrong?

Should I not have told him about the No Names rule? I wondered.

My father approached my mother, causing her to scream. He started punching her in the face with his fists, and she fell to the ground. Her face was covered in blood.

Watching my mother get beaten filled me with despair. Something in me broke. I instantly threw my small body over hers, trying to protect her.

"Stop!" I yelled. "Please stop!"

My father began to kick my mother with his boots. Then, he kicked me hard in the head. To this day, I can still feel that impact occasionally when I think of this memory.

He then dragged my mother out the door by her hair. Outside, I tried to hold her hand, determined not to let go. The whole family—my siblings—ended up in the middle of the street as they began to witness it all, just like I had.

My dad told her never to come back, and I desperately held onto her hand—until I was pulled away by my older brother, Michael.

That night, my mom left, and I didn't see her again for what felt like months.

As a child, I didn't know how to make sense of her absence. I kept wondering if it was my fault—if telling my dad about the "No Name" rule was the reason she was gone. I would stare at the front door, hoping it would open and she would walk back in. But she didn't. The silence in the house felt heavier than the violence that drove her away.

I felt abandoned and afraid—left alone with a man who had just beaten both of us.

Even though she eventually came back, something in me had changed. During that short time, my father brought home a new girlfriend—someone he would later marry. It was confusing to see her in our home, pretending like she belonged, while my mom was still gone.

Sometimes later, they were both there—my mother and my father's new girlfriend. Seeing them in the same space made everything more disorienting, like nothing in my world made sense.

Witnessing my mother being physically beaten made me more cautious. I began to hold in my words, suppress my feelings, and monitor everything I said around my father. I was terrified that anything I said might lead to her punishment—or anyone else's.

It was safer to be silent.

Safer not to feel.

Safer to disappear inside myself.

My First Time Running Away

My little 5-year-old self's life was becoming more un-safe by the day. I had learned to be cautious when talking about trafficking, and I began to lose trust in those around me.

Who is safe?

Who can I trust?

As those questions swirled in my mind, I felt there was only one thing left to do: run away from my family.

One day, while my older brother Phil was outside with me, I quietly left. I walked away from our home and began to run down the street. I made it all the way to the end of the road, where I stopped at a stop sign.

I didn't know which way to go—right or left.

Where do I go from here?

What am I going to do?

Where do I go?

I stood there for what felt like a long time. Long enough for Phil to notice and tell my father. Eventually, my dad came and found me. After that, I was severely punished for running away.

He locked me in our basement—pitch black, cold, and silent—for days. My hands were bound behind my back with a rope. I remember the hardwood floor pressing against my skin, and the ache of being stuck in that position for so long.

Then, my father repeated a Satanic ritual over me—one that reminded me of something I had endured at age two. This time, he killed a rabbit in front of me and tied it above my head. As I sat in the darkness, the blood dripped down my body.

At five years old, my parents' mission was accomplished: I was silent and submissive. Trafficking, Satanic ritual abuse, and military experiments were all happening at the same time. Fear of punishment—for myself and for others—convinced me there was no way out.

But what they couldn't destroy was the part of me that still longed for more.

Somehow, deep inside, I still believed there had to be something better than this pain. That belief—small as it was—kept a light alive in me.

The next chapter of my story isn't just about survival.

It's where hope begins to rise.

Chapter 7
Age 5 Encounter With Jesus

A few months after enduring days confined in the basement, I found myself sitting alone in the living room, watching television. My twin sister and Phil were likely playing upstairs, and my other siblings, along with my mother in the house, were probably still asleep. As I sat watching the screen, a commercial came on. It showed missionaries feeding children in Africa while sharing the Gospel of Jesus Christ.

Drawn by the stirring in my heart and soul, I walked outside and began to think of Jesus, the children in the TV commercial, and what I knew through Christmas songs.

Next to our shed, we had a flatbed trailer that I jumped on, and I began to dance and sing Christmas songs like "Holy Night" and "Away in a Manger." As I sang and danced, I stopped, looked up into the sky, and said, "Jesus! I want to be a missionary one day for you."

With no one around to share the Gospel of Jesus Christ with me, I had an encounter with Jesus and asked Him to be in my heart. I realized that Jesus

Christ is real and that what He did on the cross was true—even for me.

I felt the presence of God so tangibly, and in the stillness of that encounter, I heard Him speak to my heart: "Stand up in My name no matter what, and one day you will understand."

That moment was a cornerstone in my 5-year-old life. For the first time, I realized that trust and hope were possible, even in the midst of chaos.

If I could stand strong in Jesus, I would have hope. For the first time in my life, I felt true love—a love that was not conditional, not tied to fear or expectations, but pure and unchanging. In that heaven-touched moment, I also felt safety—a kind of safety I had never known before. It was as if Jesus Himself wrapped me in His arms, assuring me that I was not alone and that I was deeply cherished.

I was filled with excitement after my encounter with Jesus and couldn't wait to share His goodness with my siblings, parents, and anyone who would listen. But my joyful declarations about Jesus and my newfound faith were not received the way I had hoped. Instead, they brought more punishment. My father, angry and unsettled by my faith once again, became even more determined to manipulate and brainwash me through more intense ritualistic abuse, but my faith only deepened. I took heart in the words that the Lord spoke to me: "Stand up in my name no matter what, and one day you will understand."

Severe Punishments for My Faith

My life followed with even more intense suffering as my father attempted to break my faith in Jesus through relentless and horrifying punishments. After I openly shared my faith and described my encounter with Jesus, my father's actions became increasingly cruel and ritualistic.

One of the most disturbing memories right after my encounter with Jesus was when my father dug a hole in the middle of our cornfield and placed me inside a container, giving me only a water hose to breathe through. It was night, and though I don't know how long I was there, it felt like days. The experience was terrifying and dehumanizing.

There, in the silence of the earth around me, fear tried to drown out what I had known on that trailer. It made me question my encounter with Jesus. But my encounter with Him was so real. I felt His presence—still, steady—and His words were like fire that sealed my heart. I held onto what He had spoken: "Stand up in My name no matter what." That word was the anchor that kept me from falling apart. I didn't understand why things were happening the way they were, but somehow, I knew I could still trust Him.

Looking back, I see that even there—in a buried container in the middle of a field—Jesus was with me. What I had felt that day as I danced and sang wasn't a passing emotion. It was Jesus marking me with His love and His calling. And even when the darkness tried to smother that light, His love stayed. His voice never left me.

I didn't need to understand everything. I just needed to keep standing—because He was standing with me. His love was more real than the fear. His presence was more secure than the ground above me. And that has never changed.

Transition: Moving to Texas

Shortly after this, I can remember us moving to Dallas, Texas. It was a very confusing time, as living arrangements would change frequently—sometimes staying with my father, stepmother, and my two stepbrothers, and other times with my mother and brothers.

One particular time, we were living at my mother's home on Lazy River Street.

I can remember my parents nicknaming me "Retard" to mock my faith in Jesus. They encouraged my siblings to call me by this name as well and to treat me with indifference, often leaving me feeling rejected and isolated—like the only way to be accepted was to let go of Jesus. While my siblings were allowed to play outside, I was not allowed most times, though occasionally I was let out.

At times, my mother confined me indoors, locking me in her bedroom and chaining me to the bed frame.

On other occasions, I was allowed to wander through the house while my siblings played outside.

One particular night, while my siblings were outside, I noticed my mother seemed very sad. I peeked into the bathroom because I could hear her crying—and found her having sliced her wrist. She had attempted suicide. I quickly ran outside to get my older brother, Mark. He saw what I had seen and called 911.

After that night, my mother's involvement in our lives became unstable. My father would often force her to come back and care for us using manipulation and control. This led to my father taking on a more active role in our upbringing. Eventually, my mother and stepmother lived together, and then became next-door neighbors—further complicating the family dynamics and all under my father's watchful control.

To Be Continued...

As my life story continues, you will read of some of the intensified abuse and public humiliation we children endured—those of us who were trafficked and victims of satanic ritual abuse. We were often forced to watch each other's punishments to keep us silent.

Even in the darkest moments of my life, I came to understand something so beautiful and so steady: the Holy Spirit was always with me. He lived inside of me. No matter what was taken from me—no matter what my father tried to do—he could not take away my salvation. I belonged to Jesus. And nothing, not pain, not shame, not even the chains meant to silence me, could separate me from the love of Christ and the hope he gave me.

Part 2
Trafficking, Fear, and Control

Revival Fire Press

Chapter 8
Texas Sex Trafficking Ages 6-13

When we moved to Dallas, just before the start of first grade, I was only six years old. My childhood in Texas turned out to be completely different from what I had hoped—or even imagined. During those early years, my twin and I were often taken to many different places with our father. Hotels, in particular, left a lasting impression on me.

In this chapter, I will share some of the most disturbing locations we were taken to: rental lake houses, rundown motels, private residences, a military base, warehouses, underground tunnels, RV campers, and storage units.

We also spent time with a community connected to families from India. As time went on, the pattern expanded to include places like Masonic lodges, bars, and certain restaurants. Occasionally, we even traveled by plane, helicopter, or boat.

As I grew older, I began to despise my parents more deeply for the situations they placed me in. Eventually, I started running away—especially after being taken to being taken to hidden medical offices and so-called pregnancy centers.

I've held onto these fragmented but vivid memories for years. I made it a point to remember the names of places and locations, clinging to the only evidence I had of what was done to us.

Hotels: Age 6

The first memory I have of Texas begins when I was about six years old. My father took my twin and me to a shopping mall in Dallas. Inside the mall was a hotel. The shops and restaurants filled the bottom floors, and we took the elevator up to the rooms. I believe the hotel was near Dallas Airport.

Before these visits, we were dressed up. Our hair was curled and styled in matching pigtails, and we wore clean, new dresses. That wasn't normal for us. In our daily lives, we didn't pay much attention to hygiene or clothing, and we weren't allowed to wear dresses to school or anywhere else.

I remember holding my father's hand while my twin held the other. I wondered, Why can't we look like this every day?Wearing dresses, having curled hair, and receiving attention for our appearance felt surreal. It wasn't who we were—it was who they made us appear to be.

As we walked through the mall's first floor, we eventually made our way to the hotel elevators. The men I was forced to be with wore expensive business suits. We went back there many times, meeting different men during each visit. It became a repetitive routine: ride the elevator, enter a room, and obey. Sometimes my twin and I were kept together. Other times, we were separated.

These men looked important—like doctors, lawyers, or businessmen. They handed cash to my father. In return, my twin and I were used to fulfill their sexual desires. Throughout these times, I never bothered to learn the names of any of the men. Our instructions were clear—we were to refer to them only as "No Name."

One memory that stands out from our time at the airport hotel is the night I found myself alone in a room with a well-dressed man. He was drinking liquor and slurring his words, which created a terrifying, disorienting atmosphere. I believe his laughter and pretend playfulness were just a cover for the abuse he inflicted on me beneath the oversized white comforter.

In earlier visits, having my twin with me brought a small sense of comfort—we could watch out for one another. But it was also excruciating to witness her being hurt. It left me with a constant tug-of-war inside: needing her there, but wishing she didn't have to endure it either.

The sickening reality of what these men did to us became a routine part of life—something we learned to survive, even when it broke us.

The Slums: Age 7-8

My father was solely driven by money when he trafficked us. His high-end clients were usually wealthy men with powerful social or economic status. But when those men weren't available, we were still trafficked—sometimes in local slums, even in places as ordinary as a sex shop stores.

I was hyper-focused on my surroundings, always listening to the adults' conversations. I was determined to remember everything.

One time I distinctly remember being near the World Wrestling Arena in Dallas and being in close proximity to a sex toy store. Inside the store, there were separate rooms in the back, equipped with holes where men could insert their genitals. My twin and I were forced to perform oral sex on these men. We were taught that if we became proficient at this act, we wouldn't have to engage in intercourse with men as frequently. It seemed like a preferable alternative to vaginal penetration which is even disgusting to have to think that way.

As time went on, we became accustomed to the rules and regulations of the trafficking world. The slums were our training grounds. One of the first rules ingrained in us was to never make eye contact. We were told that doing so could cost us our lives. Instead, we were instructed to smile and pretend to enjoy the sexual encounters—as if our lives depended on it.

Another form of punishment and control was being burned on the bottoms of my feet by both of my parents. This was one of my earliest punishments. Over time, I began to associate those burns with eating—believing that pain would keep me thin. My father was usually the one who burned the soles of my feet as punishment. I also received burns on my back, including being branded.

France & The General

One day, my older sister came running home to my twin and me, her voice filled with excitement as she asked, "Do you want to go to France?" It sounded like a lot of fun—the idea of France felt far away and exciting. I could see the joy on my sister's face, and that made the invitation even more appealing.

But the excitement faded when I realized that "going to France" meant our father would be coming too.

We were taken to a small airport close to our hometown of Duncanville, Texas. Remember how I mentioned being hyper-focused on my surroundings—listening for names, watching for landmarks, tracking patterns and timing? I believe that small airport was no more than ten miles from where we lived, on Lazy River Drive.

My twin, our older sister, and I boarded the small airplane with our father. The two pilots were seated up front. We landed at night in an unfamiliar location—it definitely wasn't Texas. I had lost all sense of time on the plane and felt disoriented when we arrived. I suspect I was drugged, because I woke up in a tropical place where the sound of waves could be heard the moment the wheels touched the ground.

The island resembled a park, and once we landed, we didn't need a vehicle to explore. I looked around at the palm trees and the water surrounding us, marked by the steady crash of waves nearby.

As we stepped off the plane, my father was greeted by a man in a military uniform. "Hello, General," my father said, shaking his hand. His title alone—General—made him unforgettable. The uniform was a deep navy blue, adorned with gold buttons and layered with ornate gold tassels. The man appeared to be in his forties, petite in stature, about five and a half feet tall. He had thick, light gray hair, a tanned complexion, and a voice that didn't sound American to me.

In the distance, I could hear people—it sounded like a party. But the crowd was out of sight, somewhere farther from the house and closer to a bathroom area.

The inability to leave the island, combined with the shock of being in a foreign country, made my fear even more intense than it had ever been in America. I had run away before, but this time, my father warned me that the consequences here would be different. He told me that if I didn't follow instructions, I could be killed. This place, he said, was not like America.

My twin and I were then instructed to go with the General. We walked with him toward the house, while my father and older sister headed in the opposite direction—toward the people we had heard in the background, the ones who sounded like they were partying.

The General seemed especially interested in my twin. She had very blonde hair and light blue eyes—the features most sex traffickers seemed to desire. I, on the other hand, had dirty blonde hair and blue eyes. I wasn't as striking or appealing by their standards. I don't say that in a negative way—these were simply the traits that attracted sex traffickers, perpetrators, and pedophiles.

My twin always felt like a bigger target. And because of that, I always wanted to protect her. I was scared for her.

In the bedroom, after we'd entered the house, the General instructed my twin to get into bed. He had me to sit at the end of the bed and   and then he had began to lay and proceed to rape my twin. To divert his attention from my twin and ease her fears, from his back and began to hug on him and kiss his neck . This angered him so much that he kicked me off the bed with force.

As he violated my twin, I was forced to witness and watch the unspeakable acts he did to my twin before he turned his attention to me, pushing me down on the bed and subjecting me to the same abuse.

Later that night, we were taken to the party area where my father and older sister were. Multiple people were gathered outside, partying. I remember feeling indifferent.

The events that followed became a ritualistic bloodbath. People danced naked in blood, appearing drunk or drugged. Some details from that night elude me, but I distinctly remember the bathroom setup near the party area.

The outdoor bathroom featured two toilets, a handwashing station, and a single shower entrance—one I could still identify if I saw it today. The shower area was used to clean the blood from our bodies afterward. I remember seeing blood stains everywhere inside the stalls.

As our time there came to an end, my older sister was in charge of us. She made sure we cleaned ourselves in the shower and put on our clothes.

When we landed back in Texas, I remember feeling less disoriented. The drive home to Duncanville felt short, as if we were just ten minutes away—only confirming for me that the location had been close in proximity.

Although I have other vague memories of being in different cultural settings and traveling by plane, those memories remain blurry. Still, perhaps this one memory is enough to share with you.

Helicopters (AGE 11)

I remember one time when my father took my twin and me to a tall, green-glass building in downtown Dallas. From there, we boarded a helicopter. We flew north—somewhere out of state. I don't know exactly where we landed, but I remember it was cold. The land looked nothing like Texas. There were steep mountains, and the streets were made of brick or stone—pavement I had never seen before. Eventually, we landed in a grassy field near a hotel. The spot had been marked specifically for the helicopter.

When we got to the hotel, we walked through the doors and climbed a few steps. As we entered the elevator to go up, I made a split-second decision—I took off running.

I knew this might be my only chance to get away. I ran out of the hotel and down several streets. Once I realized no one was chasing me, I slowed to a walk. But as I walked, my thoughts turned to my twin.

Will she be punished because I left? Will they hurt her? Will she be killed because I ran?

The fear hit me like a wave. My stomach dropped, and I began to panic—not for myself, but for her. I turned around. I had to go back.

As I returned to the hotel, my father was already there, standing on the steps waiting for me. Calm. Collected. Like he knew I would come back.

My heart pounded. My mind raced. Where's my twin? I assumed he had already taken her up the elevator to the hotel room.

I was terrified. What was going to happen now? What had I done?

I walked with my father into the hotel room, the two men were already there—with my twin. I dropped to my knees and begged for forgiveness as I saw my twin hanging—a rope wrapped around her neck, her feet barely touching the ground on her tiptoes.

It was sickening. A video camera on a tripod was pointed directly at my naked twin. I immediately began begging again. "I'm so sorry for running. Please don't hurt her." They began to tighten the noose as my father made me watch. One of the men slapped her across the face and put a gun to her head. He pulled the trigger—but there was no bullet. Thankfully.

Then the men put me into another noose they had set up, made me strip, and forced me to stand on my tiptoes too—naked, in front of the camera That's when the man began to pornographic film. They did sadistic things to both me and my twin as the camera recorded. And just like that—it was over. Then we were flown back to Texas.

Programming: Obedience Through Fear

This became our normal. Not just abuse—conditioning.
   If I disobeyed, someone else would be hurt.
   If I ran, my twin might die.
   If Ididn't always suffer, someone else did.
   Compliance became a form of protection.
   Fear taught us to survive.
   Guilt trained us to obey.
   Love was weaponized.

Where They Took Us

Life looked like being moved, hidden, and sold—again and again.
   We were taken to lake houses , hotels, businesses
   We were sold in RVs and campers.
   Kept in private homes.
   Locked inside storage units.
   Passed through carnivals.
   Dropped at gas stations and restaurants.
   Held underground in manhole tunnels.
   And sometimes, we were kept in a small community of people who were from India.

The Boat & The Ocean (Age 13)

After my older brother Michael graduated high school, he moved to West Palm Beach, Florida. Eventually, my twin, along with my brother Phil and my mother, followed him there.

But my father had different plans for me.

While the others moved to Florida, I was still living in Theexas—kept there for trafficking.

At thirteen, I was forced on a trip and ended up on a large boat in the Atlantic Ocean, just off the coast of West Palm Beach.

The boat was sizable, with a lower deck that held a table where my father and a few other men played cards and drank beer. One of the bedrooms below deck held my twin. Past the bedrooms was an open space, blending into a small kitchenette beside the card table.

My father told me to stay in one of the rooms—his message was clear: I was expected to engage with the men.

I rebelled. I hoped my older brother would protect me.

I believed maybe—just maybe—he'd intervene.

But instead of saving me, he punished me.

Michael and another man threw me off the boat's deck into the ocean.

I was deeply disturbed that it was my own brother who had thrown me off the deck.

He wouldn't let me back on until I agreed.

I was terrified—treading water, realizing I had no control.

I thought I might drown. I couldn't outsmart anyone. There was no escape.

Eventually, my brother tossed me a life float. I was pulled back onto the boat.

Dripping and shaken, I dried off and went into the room I was told to stay in.

That night, the men took turns.

They drank beer. They played cards.

And while they laughed, they raped me repeatedly.

Following that experience in West Palm Beach, I began having more frequent panic attacks and heightened anxiety—especially around water. The fear of drowning gripped me, whether I was near a lake, a swimming pool, or any body of water. Even after returning to Texas, that fear never left me. Water no longer felt safe.

Back in Texas, the trafficking didn't stop. It continued— trafficking continued in new forms. This was my life. Even so, hope lived—holding onto the dream that I would one day break free.

Chapter 9
Satanic Occult & Military Involvement

Punishments & Fears Instilled

One night, my parents brought me and my siblings to a satanic occult gathering deep in the woods. It was here, where we had witnessed three men hanging from a tree with ropes around their necks. It was apparent that they had been murdered.

Although I did not see the actual killings, but their bodies were hanging lifeless. "These men have been accused of betraying the occult's secrets," my father, whom I believed to be the occult's leader, declared.

As an 8-year-old, I stood beside my brother Phil, who was two years older than me, feeling a mix of fear and trembling. Approximately 20 people surrounded us as my father, who had a gun in his hand as he spoke of these men.Then my father looked at me and told me to hold the pistol and aim at the men who were hanging from the tree.

Why me? I think he was trying to teach me a lesson; if I ever revealed the occult secrets, I might suffer the same fate.

I began to scream and cry. No! No!

Trembling, I curled into a fetal position on the ground, rejecting the gun.My mind began to rationalize vastly and think. I thought, "What if they were not dead, and I shot at them? Then it is all my fault. I continued to refuse to take the gun.

My father turned to my brother Phil, saying, "Since you will not do it, then your brother has to."

My brother Phil was upset and crying too, begging, " Please don't make me do it."

If you don't," said my father, then your other sister will have to (Gena, my twin).

Reluctantly, my brother held the gun and shot at the three men.

My brother must have been emotionally devastated. A terrible decision was forced upon him.He must have felt immense guilt. I felt guilty too. My hesitation forced him to shoot.My inaction caused him to carry this burden.This will stay with me forever. I always feared my brother would hate me since he was the one who shot the gun.

Seeing three men hanging dead in a tree filled us children with terror that night; it was a clear warning about the consequences of revealing occult secrets. Being forced to fire the gun destroyed a part of our innocence.

Punishing The Children: A Night to Remember

One of the most devastating traumatic events occurred when I was around age 10. This memory vividly illustrates how the satanic occult and trafficking networks operated together, using fear as a tactic—forcing children to watch the punishment of others as a method of control and intimidation.

We were standing in a wooded area, so deep among the trees that no homes or roads were visible. It felt completely isolated from the outside world. About 20 of us children were grouped together on one side, and there were roughly 100 people in total, most of them adults.

This was a meeting of the satanic occult, which constantly sought to disprove the Bible or mock scripture. As I stood with the other children, I saw a raised wooden platform positioned in front of us. The platform was built specifically for someone to stand upon. One method used to keep children silent was to select one child and publicly humiliate them in front of the others, instilling fear and reinforcing their control.

That day, I was selected as the child to be publicly humiliated and punished in front of everyone. I was told to step forward and stand on the wooden platform. My heart pounded as my father and several other adult leaders stood silently around me. These men instructed me to recite a Bible scripture clearly as they slowly dictated each word to me.

It was John 3:16, which says, "For God so loved the world that He gave His one and only Son, that whoever believes in Him shall not perish but have eternal life."

I was told to tell the crowd standing in front of me after sharing the scripture that if anyone wanted to accept Jesus Christ in their heart, to come up to the front. A man with blonde curly hair, who had looked to be in his mid-twenties of age, came up to the front of the wooded stage and bowed his head in front of me. As He put his head down pretending to pray, he then looked up at me and then he smiled. He grabbed me off the stage and within that 10-foot range of the other people and began to rape me in front of the crowd of people in front of the other children, too.

As my parents watched, they said nothing. Afterward, they had me sold to the man who raped me—for what seemed to be about two months. He lived in a small, run-down studio shack set apart from another home. I remember the main room was his bedroom, with a small kitchenette off to the side. In the center of the room, next to his bed, stood a solid white pole. During the day, he would leave and tie me to that pole with a rope, forcing me to stand there until he returned.

The man would leave his home dressed in a military uniform, making it clear where he had come from.

I remember the one window in his home—the only view to the outside. I would stare through it for hours as I stood there, tied and bound, anxious and afraid, watching for the moment he'd return. The sight of his car pulling up filled me with dread. Once he was home, he would rape me—over and over again.

During that time, he was violently abusive. He made constant threats to hurt me, to break me, to erase any sense of safety or control. He wanted me to believe I was completely his—owned, sold, and beyond help. And eventually, I did. He convinced me I belonged to him forever.

At one point, I managed to study the view outside while tied up during the hours he was gone. I watched carefully—learning the patterns, waiting for a moment. One day, when he came home and untied me, I made a quick move and ran out the front door, sprinting through the open fields.

He shouted after me, "I'll just call your dad and get your twin—she'll take your place!"

That stopped me in my tracks. I froze. The thought of him hurting my twin was worse than anything he could do to me. So, I turned around and went back. And just like that, I continued as his slave.

I was only ten years old, and this man caused deep confusion in me. He shattered my sense of identity at that time. I felt completely lost—trapped in a cycle of manipulation, fear, and repeated violations that I couldn't understand or escape.

No One To Tell

The day I was returned to my parents was marked by yet another satanic ritual. It was the moment I was transitioned back into their lives. We were once again in an open field, with a stage set up—similar to before. It might have even been the exact same one. A large bonfire burned nearby, and there were about the same number of people gathered as last time.

It felt like we were close to the man's home, but I couldn't be sure. Everything looked familiar—the texture of the grass, the feel of the ground beneath my feet—but I was disoriented. So many places blurred together in my memory, especially when fear was involved.

Here we go again—the stage. That same wooden platform I was told to stand on with four other children. It was a bit scary. I saw my parents there and thought, surely, I won't get picked. They won't let me die.

We children knew the fire was for a sacrifice. I knew one of us was going to be chosen. It felt like we were being selected for something we didn't even understand.

As we stood there on the stage, a young boy close to my age was chosen. Sadly, he was thrown into the fire and killed. It was devastating. I didn't know what to say or how to respond. I was in total shock and horror—that's the only way I can explain it.

I left with my parents afterward. I felt broken down and completely submissive to them.

Every time I remember that young boy, I can't help but wonder—who was he? Was he a foster kid? Had he run away? Who was he really? I didn't see anyone there who seemed to care for him, no one who looked like his parents. And even sadder than that—who could I even tell? The people involved were the very ones who were supposed to protect us: police officers, teachers, military personnel.

The Man Again

A few months later, we were living in Dallas, close to the Bronco Bowl, in an apartment complex nearby. My twin and I would sometimes walk about half a mile down the road to the gas station to get candy or a soda.

One day, just after leaving the gas station with the candy we'd picked out, a black Trans Am pulled up beside us. The moment I saw the driver, my stomach dropped. I recognized him instantly—it was the same man with blonde curly hair who had kept me trapped for two horrific months.

Without thinking, I grabbed my twin's arm and told her, "Follow me." He started moving toward us, trying to get closer. At the same time, I spotted a police officer parked at a nearby stoplight. I waved, hoping desperately to catch his attention, but he never looked our way.

Still, the officer's presence must have rattled the man—especially knowing I was desperately trying to get the officer's attention. He hesitated, then got back into his car and drove off.

We didn't wait. We ran from the gas station, crossed the street, and rushed into the Bronco Bowl. I figured it was the safest place—somewhere full of people. I didn't know if the man was still watching or circling nearby, so I told my twin, "Let's stay here for about twenty minutes before heading home."

When enough time had passed, we ran the rest of the way, making sure we weren't followed all the way home.

To this day, I believe if that man had managed to get us into his car, neither of us would have survived. I could feel the hatred he had for me. I'm so grateful we escaped. That day could have ended so differently.

Healing

A part of my healing that occurred later in life—especially around this memory in particular—was the realization that nothing is hidden from God.

As I cried out to Him and asked Him to share His heart with me—to show me where He was in that moment—the Lord gently responded.

He showed me that when I was up on that stage, sharing John 3:16—"For God so loved the world that He gave His one and only Son..."—the Holy Spirit was there, ministering to the children with comfort and love.

God's presence was there—and available to anyone who would receive it.

Even for that little boy who was there, and lost his life—nothing was hidden from God.

As Scripture reminds us:

> "Where can I go from your Spirit? Where can I flee from your presence? If I go up to the heavens, you are there; if I make my bed in the depths, you are there. If I rise on the wings of the dawn, if I settle on the far side of the sea, even there your hand will guide me, your right hand will hold me fast. If I say, 'Surely the darkness will hide me and the light become night around me,' even the darkness will not be dark to you; the night will shine like the day, for darkness is as light to you." Psalm 139:7–12 (NIV)

And for that young boy who lost his life, Scripture in Isaiah 49:15–16 reminds us:

"Can a mother forget the baby at her breast and have no compassion on the child she has borne? Though she may forget, I will not forget you! See, I have engraved you on the palms of my hands; your walls are ever before me." (NIV)

Even in the midst of horror, grief, and confusion—His light was present.

God never forgets. Not the unseen. Not the abused. Not the ones taken too soon.

Even when others abandon us, He does not.

And now, I live as one who is fully known, fully seen, and fully welcomed into His kingdom.

No longer hidden.

No longer forsaken.

Free.

Invitation to Salvation

As you reflect on the truth that nothing is hidden from God, I invite you to bring your hidden hurts, fears, and burdens to Jesus. He knows your story, your pain, and your struggles intimately—and He deeply cares for you. Just as the Holy Spirit ministered comfort and love to me and the other children, He longs to minister healing and hope to your heart right now.

God's love reaches into even our darkest moments, and He promises:

> "Come to me, all you who are weary and bur-dened, and I will give you rest." (Matthew 11:28)

If you long to experience this rest, forgiveness, and healing, please pray this prayer sincerely from your heart:

> "Lord Jesus, I come to You just as I am—broken and wounded. I believe You died for me and rose again to give me new life. Forgive my sins, heal my wounds, and free me from the pain of my past. Come into my heart, Lord, and be my Savior and

my strength. Thank You for seeing me, loving me, and never leaving me. I place my trust and my life into Your hands today. Amen."

If you prayed that prayer, please know that Jesus is with you now, and you have become a cherished child of God. Nothing will ever separate you from His faithful love.

> "I will never leave you
> nor forsake you." (Hebrews 13:5)

Welcome to His Kingdom, your eternal inheritance as a child of God.

The Military Experiments Continued.

But healing didn't mean the trauma stopped.

Even after moments of revelation—where I could sense God's presence or find comfort in truth—my life on earth continued to be marked by darkness, pain, and survival.

What God showed me in healing didn't erase what was still happening in the physical world.

The abuse continued.

The programming continued.

And the military experiments didn't stop.

As I've shared in earlier chapters, my involvement in military programming began in Tennessee with the observatory men when I was just two years old. That programming continued into my teenage years in Texas. It was difficult to separate the occult from the military—they seemed so interconnected. Both were structured, secretive, and cruel.

Unfortunately, the illegal experiments didn't stop.

I remember being hunted through the woods by a large group of men, then shot with a tranquilizer gun. This wasn't a one-time event. It happened repeatedly, almost ritualistically, as if it were a game they enjoyed playing. Each time I was caught, it deepened the fear. It tightened the grip of control they held over me.

The Hulk experiments didn't stop either. What I called mind control used fear, psychological manipulation, and torment to gain control over me. It created an internal alarm system—programming me to follow orders without question.

For example, missing a designated time—whether it was 11:30 p.m. or between 2 and 3 a.m.—meant punishment. Over time, this method of conditioning trained me to comply through fear.

Example of Conditioning and Mind Programming

When I was around nine years old, I began having repeated memories of waking up in the middle of the night and walking to a park behind our home. That park became the site of frequent gatherings involving Satanists—and my father. At this time in my life, I was living in my father's home, not with my mother. These events were not isolated; they were part of something more coordinated, involving both the Satanic occult and military personnel.

This is where the mind programming began to take deeper root. I associated specific objects and symbols as triggers—what I came to understand as tools of conditioning. For example, a location marked by an "X"—as in "X marks the spot"—or a POW (Prisoner of War) sign would immediately activate a mental response. These symbols weren't random. They were intentionally used to provoke fear, submission, or a programmed response to follow an instruction. Red lights were another frequent trigger. These associations were not natural—they were created through deliberate conditioning on or near military bases and in occult settings.

Sometimes the programming experiments felt unreal—like I had to leave my body just to survive it. One of the most terrifying techniques involved having water poured over my face—something I now understand to be waterboarding. These sessions were often accompanied by other forms of physical and psychological torment: electric shocks, repeated exposure to hypnotic or disturbing tape recordings, and being submerged underwater as part of experimental conditioning.

I was also exposed to extreme sensory overload—like aggressive, high-volume music blasted at unbearable levels. These experiences weren't accidental. They were designed to destabilize me—physically, emotionally, and mentally.

Texas Military Experiments

One particular military experiment I remember took place near our home in the Dallas, Texas, area. The dirt roads winding through the military base are vivid in my memory—small ditches ran along the sides, and a line of trees stretched along the path as you drove. Various turnoffs along those roads led to different areas of the base. It was there that military personnel carried out illegal experiments that pushed my body far beyond its limits.

This new phase of experimentation focused specifically on my athletic abilities. Because of my natural talent in sports, they designed a program to make me stronger, faster, and more resilient—pushing the limits of my physical capabilities as part of their testing.

Growing up, my twin and I were fortunate to have a next-door neighbor named Sammy, who became our best friend. Her parents took a genuine interest in caring for us and often stepped in to support us—including rides to and from soccer games and practices. During our elementary school years, Sammy, my twin, and I all tried out for soccer, which led us to play recreationally and, eventually, at the competitive classic level.

You may wonder how I was even allowed to play soccer in the midst of all this. I always wondered about that myself. Maybe it was just a way to make our lives appear normal—like a carefully placed mask to cover the chaos underneath.

By the time I was twelve, I had earned a spot on the Texas state traveling soccer team—a significant milestone in my athletic journey. But I couldn't play. Sammy, whose family had always been our transportation and support system, didn't make the team. Without her, I had no way to get to practices or games. It was heartbreaking because soccer had become an emotional outlet for me. It boosted my confidence and gave me a sense of identity.

As my father recognized my athletic potential, he found ways to exploit it. He turned my physical abilities into another opportunity for financial profit—yet another way to use me for his own gain.

Project Miles

At the age of twelve, this period marked the beginning of what I would later call Project Miles. My physical talents and intelligence were targeted and tested as part of a larger effort to push me beyond my limits.

These tests weren't just physical—they placed me in impossible situations that forced me to think fast, adapt, and survive under extreme pressure. Over time, a dissociative identity began to emerge—Miles. She was intelligent, calculated, and capable of excelling in high-stress challenges. She didn't just endure—she outmaneuvered.

Miles developed unique strategies to protect me. One of those strategies included keeping information hidden from the Hulk part of me to avoid "reporting." In the internal structure of my mind, this was a survival tactic. The less Hulk knew, the less that could be used against me. This split between parts of me wasn't random; it was a defense mechanism born from necessity. These human experiments were not isolated acts of cruelty—they were designed to test the extremes of what the mind could endure and adapt to under relentless trauma.

Fighting Games

One of the most disturbing psychological games they used involved forcing participants to fight one another—until one person was no longer able to stand. Sometimes that meant fighting strangers. Other times, it meant fighting my own twin.

My parents had always tried to create strife between my twin and me growing up. In these controlled fights, there was no room for emotion. The rules were simple: the fight wouldn't end until someone was knocked out. The fear of seriously injuring someone I loved was overwhelming. And yet, I was forced to push past that fear.

The beatings were often severe. I remember being thrown into ice baths after losing consciousness or going into shock. People would massage my body, trying to bring me back—and somehow, I always came back. I shouldn't have survived some of those moments, but I did.

These episodes weren't just physical torture—they were deeply psychological. was forced to repeat back phrases that had been implanted in my mind while electrodes were attached to my body. The purpose was always the same: to break me, to shape me, and to program me.

I often felt like a lab animal. A mouse in a maze, constantly tested to see how far I could go, how much I could endure, how quickly I would adapt under pressure. I wasn't just surviving—I was being conditioned.

Finding Meaning in the Chaos

How do I make sense of these experiences? At first glance,they seem senseless—just a series of cruel, inhuman experiments.

But beneath the horror, I began to see something else: the strength of my mind to protect itself, to survive, and to adapt.

Each layer of mind programming, each identity that emerged,was not a failure—it was a strategy.

My mind was doing everything it could to shield me from what no child should ever have to endure.

Survival became the proof that God had not abandoned me—even when I couldn't feel Him.

And that, in its own way, is a kind of miracle.

Part 3
God's Love

Revival Fire Press

Chapter 10
Awakened Love

In middle school, I was active in sports—I played soccer, ran track, and participated in tennis. In 8th grade, a friend invited me to church, and I began attending youth group on Wednesday nights.

Around that same time, I also began experimenting with illegal drugs as a way to self-medicate, along with two boys from my school, Chris and John, who lived on my street. Unlike in my trafficking experiences, where drugs were forced on me, this was a choice I made on my own.

One night, Chris, John, and I walked to a bridge near the church where I attended youth services. Just before the panic attack, we smoked marijuana under the bridge—laced with something unknown. It triggered a severe panic attack, and I felt like I was dying.

Overcome with fear, I ran to the church, desperate for comfort. When I arrived, the building was empty. In my desperation, I cried out in prayer: "Jesus, please forgive me.

If you let me live, I will dedicate my life to you." I meant every word.

At five years old, I had a powerful encounter with Jesus. I heard Him say: "Stand up in His name no matter what. One day, you will understand." That moment had stayed with me through the years. Now, in my desperation, I didn't just remember it—I wondered if God was calling me deeper, inviting me into something more intimate than I'd ever known.

I was taken to a hospital to be evaluated for my drug use. The day after my hospital release, I met with the youth pastors. I remember kneeling at the altar, crying as they prayed with me. It was a moment of deep peace—the most resounding cry of my young life at 13. My eyes opened in a new way—not to love Jesus for the first time, but to love Him beyond fear. I felt His loving presence again, just like I had as a child. That mercy changed me.

At home, I started reading the Bible for hours at night, sitting outside while my brother Phil hosted beer parties inside. Those quiet moments with God became some of my favorite memories. I poured my heart into my relationship with Jesus Christ, my Savior.

A Dream That Spoke the Truth

It was during one of those nights that I had a vivid dream—one that left a lasting impression. In the dream, I was asleep on the couch in our living room. Suddenly, the devil appeared—a three-foot-tall figure—walking through the room. His presence filled me with intense fear and intimidation. I was struck by how someone so small could provoke such overwhelming dread. In the dream, I grabbed a Bible and began reading it out loud. As I read, the front door opened, and a pastoral man entered with a bright light. The devil immediately fled, and the eerie "sanctuary room" next to the living room— a room my father used for ritual abuse— transformed into a beautiful garden. That dream confirmed the power of God's Word and His ability to drive out darkness.

As my faith deepened, my father began to notice the changes in me. Not long after, he forced me to go on a sudden trip to Tennessee with him. I found myself trapped in a horrifying situation. We arrived at a rundown building, surrounded by red, muddy dirt roads. Inside, I saw my paternal grandparents, along with other individuals involved in what I now recognize as occult practices.

I was restrained with thick ropes, my wrists and ankles tightly bound, and endured excruciating physical torment. Satanic rituals were performed over me, marking the beginning of extreme spiritual warfare in my life. At such a young age, I couldn't fully comprehend what was happening, but the spiritual and emotional aftermath was overwhelming.

When Words Weren't Enough

When we returned to Texas, I continued to keep the experiences of trafficking and abuse a secret. Despite my silence, I tried to seek help from the youth pastors, as I was still having nightmares and what I can only describe as spiritual torment. Unfortunately, the youth pastors misunderstood my struggles. The truth of my life was too complex to explain—I couldn't find the words to describe the pain of trafficking and abuse. To make matters worse, my father manipulated the situation, calling them and convincing them I was lying about him.

They, in turn, tried to reassure me of my father's love for me, completely unaware of the reality I was living in. Through it all, I clung to my faith. God's presence remained my anchor, even in the midst of indescribable pain. The raw spiritual warfare and the concept of deep intimacy of God's love were enough to sustain me, yet my heart stayed guarded. The mind programming and self-preservation I had developed over time were still strong.

Even though I stubbornly stood firm in Jesus, I struggled to fully embrace intimacy with His love. Deep down, I feared that opening myself to that closeness might make me vulnerable—that His love could somehow be taken away.

Even in my guarded state, I knew one truth for sure: God had never abandoned me. His love was constant, and His hand was guiding me—even as I was still learning to trust Him more deeply.

Cancer: An Unexpected Journey

My life took an unexpected turn after eighth grade. During the summer, I frequently complained to my mother about stomach pain and pelvic discomfort. Despite the discomfort, I tried to push through as summer ended and ninth grade began. I was excited about this new chapter of high school—especially since I had made the ninth-grade soccer team and had even been promoted to play for the junior team as a freshman.

One day, while sitting in class, I began to feel nauseous. I raised my hand and asked my teacher if I could go to the restroom. As I walked down the hall, I suddenly began vomiting. Someone noticed and quickly came to help, guiding me to the nurse's station at the front of the school. I remember the principal being there, trying to comfort me and asking questions while I continued to throw up a yellow liquid

Soon, my older sister showed up at the school to pick me up and rushed me to the hospital. After running some tests, the doctors found a tumor the size of a football. It was shocking. When my parents arrived, they looked concerned—but the first thing they did was start questioning me in front of the doctor.

"Are you pregnant? Are you pregnant?"

I said firmly, "No," but inside, I was terrified.

The only encounters I'd ever had were the ones they forced on me. The thought of being pregnant shook me to my core. I felt exposed, confused, and scared in a way I couldn't even explain.

That same day, I underwent emergency surgery. The doctors removed the tumor, along with my left ovary and fallopian tube. They confirmed the tumor was cancerous. What followed was a journey through chemotherapy—four sessions total. My father came to every appointment and threatened me not to say anything to the doctor. I felt like I was being watched the whole time.

The experience with cancer changed me profoundly. It left me feeling fragile, like my strength and resilience had been stripped away. Looking back, I couldn't help but wonder if the cancer was somehow connected to the trauma I had endured as a child—years of repeated sexual abuse and violations that left scars far deeper than anyone could see.

God Is at Work

Even in the darkest moments, I've come to see that God's hand is never far.

> As Philippians 1:6 says, "Being confident of this, that he who began a good work in you will carry it on to completion until the day of Christ Jesus." (NIV)

After surviving cancer, I found myself seeking refuge in unexpected places—a bowling alley, the streets, and eventually, a place called the Rockatorium.

It had only been a few months since cancer turned my world upside down, and there I was—sitting outside the bowling alley near my mom's house—when a lowrider pickup truck pulled up. A young man, slightly older than me, asked if I wanted to go to the Rockatorium with him.

Without much thought, I said yes—I didn't know what boundaries were back then. We drove a few miles to a spot where teenagers hung out behind a building near a church. There was a volleyball court outside where people played or stood around their cars talking. Inside, there were video games, pool tables, and places to hang out. On Wednesday nights, they held youth services led by youth pastors—a space for teens to gather and connect.

I began attending youth services on Wednesday nights and spent almost every day at the youth center. A lot of transitions were happening in my life. During this time, my brother Phil and Twin moved to Florida to be with my older brother, Michael. Soon after, my mother—the one I was living with—also moved to Florida. My stepbrothers, along with their mother, moved back to Tennessee to be near their family.

That left my father, my older sister Anna, and me living in Texas. I didn't want to go to my father's house on the other side of town, so I slept wherever I could on the safer streets. I was only reported as a runaway when they needed to find me for their purposes. Sometimes, I'd be gone for three or four weeks before being "called in as a runaway."

I didn't trust the police either—I had recognized some of them as being involved in sex trafficking. There were a few officers who I believe genuinely wanted to help, but I was too scared to tell the truth. I feared they might tell the wrong person—someone connected to the police or the occult—and I'd face unimaginable consequences for speaking out.

The Rockatorium became a safe haven for me—a place where teenagers gathered to play games, hang out, and attend youth services. Some nights, I began sleeping on the side of the building just to avoid going home. When the youth pastors found out, they offered me something that changed my life: a place to stay in their home.

These youth pastors were different from the ones I had known earlier in the chapter. With them, I was given a second chance—to grow in my faith, and slowly, to begin trusting again. They didn't pressure or dismiss me. They welcomed me. And even though my heart was still guarded, something in me dared to believe that maybe God hadn't forgotten me after all.

Life in their home was full of love, structure, and something I had rarely experienced—sitting down to eat meals together. I loved it. These people were the perfect example of a family. For the first time in a long time, I felt safe.

Most of me wanted to embrace it all—the stability, the kindness, the way they welcomed me without judgment. But part of me held back.

What if I let my guard down and get hurt again?

What if I give my heart to this family, to this hope, and it all gets taken away?

I was afraid that if I allowed myself to fully believe in the good, and it didn't last, I'd lose the little bit of hope I was still holding onto. So even in the comfort of their home, I stayed guarded—not because I didn't want love or trust, but because I didn't know if my heart could survive another betrayal.

Still, something was changing in me—slowly, quietly. It felt like the beginning of awakened love.

Chapter 11
Life With The Youth Pastors

Even though I loved the warmth of the youth pastors' home—the meals, the prayer, the feeling of family—I never felt fully at ease. Fear was always with me.

As a teenager, I only shared surface-level details about the abuse from my biological parents. My father knew I was staying with the youth pastors and their daughters. Outwardly, he acted fine—but only to protect his image. Pretending everything was normal helped him avoid getting caught. Behind the scenes, the threats continued. He warned me that if I spoke up, they'd hurt the family and destroy the Rockatorium.

That fear kept me guarded. I wanted to trust and love, but I couldn't risk putting anyone in danger. Survival meant staying distant and detached.

I made plenty of mistakes while living with the pastoral family—sneaking out at night to hang out with friends, getting drunk with other teens, and testing boundaries I didn't fully understand. Despite all of it, they were incredibly forgiving. They always welcomed me back and gave me the freedom to choose whether I wanted to stay or leave. In those moments, they treated me like one of their own, and through them, I began to understand what love could look like.

Still, I held back. The threats were always in the back of my mind, making it hard to let anyone in too closely.

What No One Saw

Even during the season I lived with the youth pastoral family—when I was supposed to be safe—trafficking still continued. I was still being taken, still being hurt, while my father had full access to me. The pastoral family didn't know. It was all hidden in plain sight. I learned how to live in both worlds—one where kindness was real, and one where cruelty never slept.

Sometimes I was kept in a storage unit—tied up and bound—until my father was ready to sell me. I was trafficked in a variety of places: restaurants, private homes, warehouses, lake houses, bars, Lions Clubs, carnivals, and Masonic lodges. There were even underground tunnel systems and brothels filled with older men near a VA bar.

I was also taken to secret locations for medical exams—to check if I was pregnant or had infections. Other hidden places were used when pregnancies weren't allowed to continue. One time, I saw bottles containing fetuses. That image never left me.

College & Movement

Despite everything I had endured, there were still moments when I felt movement—like something in my life was shifting, even if just slightly. While the abuse and threats hadn't completely stopped, I also began to experience glimpses of normalcy and hope. One of those turning points came when I started living more consistently with a pastoral family who offered stability and encouragement.

During that time, I rejoined a Classic League soccer team, returned to high school, and eventually earned my GED to fast-track my diploma. My teammates were focused on college, and when we heard that scouts were watching our games, I started to consider that path too.

I received soccer scholarships from a few colleges. I wanted to feel like I was moving forward, like my teammates were—so I accepted a four-year soccer scholarship in Iowa. I was proud of what I'd accomplished. Even more, the pastoral family was proud of me too.

Between Comfort and Change

Even with a scholarship in hand, I felt completely clueless about what it meant to be a college student or what lay ahead. I remember standing in my dorm room, looking at my nearly empty closet. I had only a few outfits—and it brought back painful memories of going to school as a child wearing dirty clothes, repeating the same outfit over and over. So embarrassing, I thought. I was too afraid—and too proud—to ask anyone for help.

Our university's soccer team had a dress code for away games. We were expected to wear dresses when arriving at other schools. The idea of asking for clothes felt overwhelming. Shame and vulnerability crept in, making it nearly impossible to speak up.

Before classes began, soccer practice started—and I genuinely enjoyed that part. But when it came to academics, I didn't even know what to expect. Fear of failure took over. Eventually, I made the decision to leave and return to Texas.

Back to Texas

When I got back, I found out the youth pastors I had been living with were planning to move to Missouri. Their home had always been a place I could return to—coming and going as I needed. But now, at 19 years old, I didn't know what to do with my life. Hanging out at the Rockatorium forever wasn't an option. My friends were growing up and moving on. The pastors invited me to come with them to Missouri, but I chose to stay in Texas.

I started partying and drinking almost every night while working as a server at Olive Garden. I lived wit a kind older man named Robert, who worked at a gas station. One night, sitting in a lawn chair outside his house, I found myself wondering what direction my life was headed.

A Crossroads of Conviction

Eventually, I decided to leave Texas and join the pastoral family in Missouri. They were still willing to welcome me into their home—but deep down, I didn't want to give up smoking and drinking. I struggled with the tension, especially feeling the conviction of the Holy Spirit in their home. I realized I couldn't keep hiding my self-destructive habits, so I made the choice to leave.

Chapter 12
Revival

R emembering that my older sister Anna had recently moved to Pensacola, Florida, I decided to take a road trip to visit her. On the way, I stopped at a gas station to fill up my tank.

While I was pumping gas, a man approached me and asked, "Have you been to the Brownsville Revival?"

I said, "No."

"Then you should go," he replied.

At the time, I didn't fully understand what the word revival meant, but his words stuck with me. I began to wonder what it was all about. He shared his testimony of encountering the power and presence of God during the Brownsville Revival, and something in his story stirred my heart.

Encountering God's Presence

A few days later, I found myself standing outside Brownsville Assembly of God, joining a long line of people waiting for hours to enter the church. What struck me most wasn't just the crowd—it was their joy. People were worshiping with such passion, spontaneously breaking into songs of praise as we stood together.

When the doors opened and I stepped inside the sanctuary, I was overwhelmed by the tangible presence of God. I couldn't explain it, but it felt like the weight of years' worth of pain and fear melted away in that moment. I remember running to the altar that first night, tears streaming down my face, surrendering my life to God. As I prayed and repented, I could feel a shift within me. It was as though the chains I'd carried my whole life were breaking, and the darkness that had gripped me was leaving my body. I tasted freedom for the first time—and I didn't want to leave God's presence. I wanted to live in it forever.

Breakthrough and Inner Conflict

I began attending the revival every night, soaking in God's love and allowing His presence to transform me. But as layers of past trauma began to surface, it felt like a tug of war inside me. On one hand, I was experiencing freedom in Christ. On the other, painful memories I had long buried began rising up, bringing with them waves of fear and anguish.

During this time, I stayed with my sister—but her home wasn't a safe place. Her husband was connected to the same group of human traffickers and satanic occult that my father had been involved with. I felt

trapped—torn between my longing to stay in Pensacola and my urgent need for safety.

A New Direction: Teen Challenge

I heard Evangelist Steve Hill share his testimony about
a place called Teen Challenge, where he had overcome addiction and grown in his faith. His story deeply
resonated with me, and I decided to join a Teen Challenge program in South Florida—hundreds of miles
away from my sister.

The transition wasn't easy. West Palm
Beach—where my mother, twin, and brothers
lived—was also a hub of trafficking activity tied to my
past. Memories of my parents' threats haunted me,
especially one about a so-called "death date" when
I turned 21—a date connected to the satanic occult.
Ironically, I had just turned 21 when I entered Teen
Challenge.

Learning to Heal

Teen Challenge provided structure and safety. It was
a place where I could begin to heal, grow in faith,
and develop the discipline I needed to rebuild my life.
We were taught life skills, worked hard, and studied
God's Word. During my time there, we often traveled
to churches to share testimonies of what God had
done in our lives.

When it came time to share my story, I often gave a watered-down version—talking about my struggles with living on the streets, staying with youth pastors, using alcohol, and eventually finding my way to the Brownsville Revival, where everything changed.

But I couldn't bring myself to share the darkest parts—being trafficked by my parents, enduring satanic ritual abuse, and living in constant fear. I thought that by keeping those parts hidden, I could move on.

The Struggle to Feel

Deep down, I knew the wounds were still there. I longed to forget the pain completely, convincing myself that ignoring it would somehow make it go away. But healing doesn't work that way.

Healing doesn't come by pretending the pain never happened—it comes by feeling it, facing it, and letting God into the places we've tried to hide.

But the truth was—I struggled to feel. I had spent so many years numb, detached, and in survival mode that even love or safety felt dangerous.

In order to heal, you have to feel. And I was just beginning to learn how.

Brownsville Revival School of Ministry

After completing Teen Challenge, I moved back to Pensacola, Florida—where the Brownsville Revival had taken place. There, I discovered the Brownsville Revival School of Ministry (BRSM), applied, and was accepted as a student. I started working, attending classes, and going to revival services regularly. I felt a strong sense of God's calling on my life and was hungry for more of Him.

Still Guarded

One challenge was that my older sister still lived in Pensacola. Like many trauma survivors, I didn't yet understand the importance of boundaries—I didn't even know what they were. I also kept in contact with the pastoral family but stayed at a distance, visiting them only during holidays. Even then, I remained protective—watchful, cautious, and unsure how to fully let my guard down.

Starting school, I felt overwhelmed with fear. I was stuck between wanting to feel safe and wanting to run. Danger felt more familiar to me than peace, and after so many years of control, I didn't know how to trust my instincts. My sister's husband was still connected to the trafficking network, and that fear stayed with me. If I tried to break free, I feared others might get hurt. I wanted out, but survival kept me stuck. Even small choices felt too risky.

Looking back, I can see my sister may have been keeping tabs on me—though I didn't want to admit it at the time. I convinced myself that keeping some distance, especially from the pastoral family, would protect them. That fear made me withdraw. I wanted healing and connection, but I stayed guarded. I thought if I buried the truth deep enough, I could move on and protect everyone. But silence doesn't make trauma disappear.

First & Second Semester of School

At the start of my time at BRSM, trafficking happened again. My father knew exactly how to manipulate my vulnerabilities—my faith, my love for Jesus, and my deep longing to see him come to Christ. When he found out I was attending school and the Brownsville Revival, he came into town from Texas. Around that same time, my mother and twin sister arrived from South Florida to stay with my older sister. I didn't realize it then, but something was being orchestrated.

Despite everything, I still wanted to believe there was hope for my father. I desperately longed for him to be saved and walk away from the darkness he was part of. He played on that desire, using it to pull me back in. One night, he even attended a Brownsville Revival service with me.

During the service, a man approached my father and shared his testimony—how he had been addicted to cocaine and was completely set free by Jesus. I felt encouraged, thinking maybe God was reaching my father's heart. But suddenly, in the middle of worship, he insisted we leave. I believe God's presence was confronting him, and that's exactly why he wanted to go.

After that night, something changed. He became angry—agitated by how much I had changed. It was like the light in me irritated the darkness in him. And then he did what he always did to regain control.

He drugged me.

I don't remember everything. I know he used a towel soaked in something that knocked me out. When I came to, I was in the middle of another horrific scene—a ritual involving my family and others I didn't recognize. It was filled with blood, alcohol, and unspeakable acts. It was evil. And I was right back in it.

By my second semester, I moved into an apartment complex near the school with several other BRSM students. At first, it seemed safer. But the following semester, I moved into a rental home that my older sister had suggested—a decision I thought was wise at the time. I trusted that she was trying to help me, but it ended up placing me—and the other students who lived there—right in the middle of a nest of occultic people and traffickers.

Trafficking began happening more frequently, sometimes even involving my best friend from the Brownsville Revival. I couldn't make sense of it all—it was happening too fast. I felt completely trapped, frozen by fear, unsure of how to escape.

Moments of Captivity During Ministry School

Even while I was attending the Brownsville Revival School of Ministry, the trafficking didn't stop. What was supposed to be a season of spiritual growth and safety became yet another place where abuse continued—hidden beneath the surface. These are just some of the instances I now recognize from that time:

> The Lighthouse – A location where satanic ritual abuse occurred. My father, mother, twin, older sister, and many others were present

> Trafficking Site Near the School – A building that looked like a home but was actually used for trafficking. My best friend and I remembered another young person being targeted there

> Motor Home by the Woods – Located near the school. My father was present.

My Older Sister's Backyard – My best friend and I were drugged. My father dragged me deeper into the backyard and began covering me with leaves. I was numb and paralyzed from drugs. He told me he was going to set me on fire. My best friend was tied to a tree. Then I was tied beside her.

Cantonment, Florida (Military Personnel) – A mock wedding ceremony took place involving my older sister and military men. I was beaten because I refused to eat a sacrifice or drink blood.

Hotel Near Pensacola Beach – I was sold for sex in a high-rise hotel. They threatened to throw me off the balcony if I didn't comply.

James and Jenna's Home – Neighbors involved in trafficking. They were connected with my father, sister, and military personnel.

Being trafficked alongside my best friend, we eventually made a police report. But nothing ever came of it—not even a follow-up. I remember thinking, If the police won't help, then who will?

Facing Trauma and Seeking Help

One turning point for me at school was a class on freedom in Christ, deliverance, and healing. We talked about things like abstinence, breaking past sexual ties, repentance, and letting go of fear, anger, resentment, and unforgiveness. During one of the sessions, we were invited to come up for prayer. When it came time to deal with anger, I could barely move. I struggled. Just admitting I was angry felt too big—like if I let it out, I wouldn't be able to handle it.

As time went on, I started noticing changes in myself—emotional instability and a growing urge to numb out or self-medicate. These red flags didn't line up with the person I was trying to become, and I knew deep down something wasn't right. So I reached out for pastoral counseling at the school.

During this time, I also began meeting with BRSM's deliverance and inner healing team. That's when something unexpected started happening—I began to dissociate. I would refer to myself by different names, like "Hulk" and "Tag," which were tied to darker parts of my past. For the first time, I admitted out loud that I had experienced both dissociation and sexual abuse.

The ministry team handled it with so much care and gentleness. They didn't push—they simply walked with me through it. Eventually, they encouraged me to see a professional Christian psychologist. It was during those sessions that I first learned what I now understand to be Dissociative Identity Disorder (DID)—what used to be called multiple personality disorder.

Learning about DID helped me make sense of things. The different names, the fragmented memories—it was my brain's way of surviving trauma I couldn't process as a child. DID is a complex condition that often stems from severe early childhood trauma. It's a coping mechanism where someone develops separate identity states or "alters" to handle overwhelming pain. These parts aren't "made up"—they emerge to help carry what feels unbearable.

I agree with trauma expert Bessel van der Kolk, who says that while dissociation may become maladaptive later in life, in the beginning, it can be the very thing that keeps someone alive. [1]For me, dissociation became a bridge. It helped me start naming the abuse and slowly piece together my story so I could begin to heal.

My Counseling Experience

I started seeing a Christian psychologist once a week, and he helped me more than I ever expected. In the beginning, I was like a scared dog—traumatized and unsure if I could trust anyone. It took a long time before I felt even a little bit safe with him. But over time, something began to shift. He helped me realize how hard my traffickers had worked to keep me quiet—to keep the truth hidden.

I started facing things I didn't want to feel. There were so many layers—shame, guilt, fear, abandonment. Deep down, I still believed I was bad, unlovable, dirty, and not good enough. Most of those beliefs came from how I was treated growing up.

But God didn't give up on me. He started peeling those layers back, slowly. And honestly, He's still doing that in me today.

Journaling

While I was at BRSM, one of my roommates gave me my first journal. I normally didn't keep stuff like that—anything that made me feel too much, I avoided. But for some reason, I kept that journal. And it became a lifeline.

I didn't even know what to write at first. But I started pouring my heart out—my prayers, my pain, the little glimpses of hope I was holding onto. Writing helped me deal with things I wasn't ready to say out loud. It gave me space to breathe, to process, and to start letting God work in those hidden places.

I've held onto that journal for over 25 years. What I'm about to share are two entries I wrote back then, during my time at the school—while I was still being trafficked.

Journal Entry April 23, 2001

Dear Jesus, I love you so much.

Thank you for putting people in my life to help me through. Jesus, if my dad comes and gets me. I will not be scared.

Psalm 27:1 says, "The Lord is my light and my salvation—whom shall I fear? The Lord is the stronghold of my life— of whom shall I be afraid (NIV)". You are my Father. You will protect me. Even if I die- I am going to be with you.

Save my dad, Jesus! Set him free. Holy Spirit, I want to depend on you. Do not let me do things in my own strength. May your name Jesus be glorified through this. I worship you. May I decrease so you can increase. Glory and honor and praise to you forever, Jesus. By life or by death, your servant.

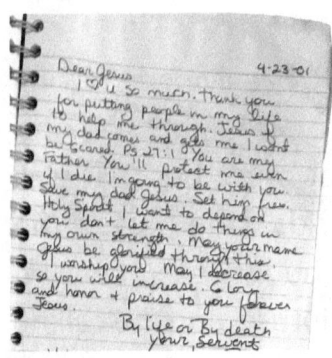

Journal Entry April, 25, 2001

Dear Jesus, Thank you for the goodnight sleep. Thank you for listening to my hearts cry. Only you can do this. Only you can change things. Thank you for giving me boldness and courage. I am in class right now...I wonder... What do you want me to do with my life? Will I even make it? Psalm 136-1 "Give thanks to the Lord, for he is good. His love endures forever."(NIV)

This was the thought process I was living in during my time at the school of ministry. It might seem impossible to hold both realities at once, but that was my life—torn between two worlds. One part of me was desperately pursuing God, hungry to know Him more, pressing into worship, Scripture, and the calling I believed He had placed on my life. I was in class, journaling prayers, memorizing Psalms, and asking God what He wanted to do with me.

At the same time, I was still being trafficked.

Football Experiments

Following my second year and graduation from BRSM, I continued counseling and started a third-year internship at the school. During this time, I was scouted while playing in an adult soccer league to try out for the Women's National Football team that had just launched in Pensacola. I didn't know much about American tackle football, but I accepted the invitation and made the team. My position became outside linebacker and special teams. We grew in popularity—often followed by the news media—and crowds showed up regularly to watch us play.

But something else was happening during this time—something I didn't know how to explain.

This is where the military experiments began again, but this time, they failed in their goal to produce a "super athlete." While playing professional football, I started feeling clumsy, less confident, and increasingly unsure of myself—as if the programming had backfired. I didn't want to become who the programmers were trying to create, so I became the opposite. It was deeply unsettling. I didn't know who to tell, and honestly, I was too terrified to say anything to anyone.

Coercion and Control

One memory that still haunts me involved being taken to an apartment building by two young military personnel and a retired CIA agent. I knew the two men were from the military because they were in uniform. Something was said that made me realize the older man—a retired CIA agent—was in charge, and that this apartment was his.

I remember the carpeted steps leading to the second floor. The CIA agent walked with a limp as we climbed. Once inside, my hands were bound behind my back, and they sat me in a chair. Then they showed me a picture of my young niece. The agent warned me: if I didn't comply with their orders, my niece would be hurt—or worse

They later took me to the bathroom. That's when they began pouring water over my face. It felt like I was suffocating. I was being waterboarded. Terrified, I submitted. I listened carefully to their instructions, which included following their programming orders to become a high-performing athlete. Part of this was running six miles toward the BRSM campus—mostly at night, around 10 p.m.—as part of a control strategy.

That path became traumatic for me. It was along that route that some of the other events I've shared took place. Over time, even hearing a whistle while jogging would trigger me, sending me into hypervigilance and anxiety.

Military Experiments Resurface

Even while playing football and attending counseling, the trafficking and military experiments hadn't stopped. I was still being targeted—and I didn't fully understand it yet. It was like I was caught in a psychological maze, constantly trying to survive while also trying to heal. I felt like I was always one step behind, using trauma responses—numbing out, disconnecting, or shutting down—to make it through.

I had begun weekly therapy sessions, doing my best to work through the trauma. But healing felt nearly impossible while I was still surrounded by traffickers. What I didn't realize at the time was that there was something even more organized—more systematic—happening behind the scenes.

In the next chapter, I begin to uncover what I now know to be an extensive network of control and exploitation, one that operated right under the surface of my daily life.

---

1. Van der Kolk, B. A. (2014). The body keeps the score: Brain, mind, and body in the healing of trauma. New York: Viking.

Chapter 13

Escape & The Cycle of Control

Unmasking the Network

As I played football, I was still under the thumb and pressure of military experiments, being trafficked, and satanic ritual abuse. On the outside, it might have looked like things were going well—I was going to counseling, trying to rebuild my life—but the truth was, I was still being targeted.

These traffickers were relentless. It was as if it were a game of cat and mouse, and there were ten cats and I was the only mouse.

Only later did I begin to grasp the extent of the manipulation and psychological control I was under. I was still relying on trauma responses just to survive—numbing out, shutting down, or disconnecting when things became too overwhelming. It felt like I was always one step behind, unable to reach a place where I could fully confront my deepest fears, even during that time.

Even as I attended counseling once a week, working through my trauma with my therapist, the cycle of abuse continued. Even as I attended counseling once a week, working through my trauma with my therapist, the cycle of abuse continued. My neighbor, who was a part of the organized trafficking, would gain information about my counseling. I later learned he was connected to my father and the military.

I was fighting to heal while simultaneously being retraumatized, trapped in a reality where progress felt impossible. I was surrounded by traffickers.

The Organized Network & Systemic Trafficking

This was not an isolated event; it was systemic trafficking involving multiple levels of perpetrators, each with specific responsibilities.[1] The Primary Perpetrators made decisions that activated Secondary Perpetrators whenever they saw fit.

Primary Perpetrators

Father and Mother

They were my main abusers—the ones closest to me, who established the abusive environment. They made the key decisions and directed others as necessary.

Common Roles Among Primary Perpetrators

Handlers: Monitored and controlled victims, ensuring they did not escape or seek help.

Logistics Coordinators: Arranged transportation and movements to advance the trafficking operation.

Enforcers: Used threats, violence, or intimidation to maintain strict control over the victim.[2]

Secondary Perpetrators

Military personnel or those who worked in government

Satanic occult leaders

Other high-ranking organizers (including those in secretive societies like Masonry)[3]

These individuals operated on a broader scale—overseeing surveillance, managing multiple victims, and coordinating the actions of lower-level perpetrators. The Primary Perpetrators would call upon them to leverage their resources, influence, or specialized roles within the network—or to track me down if needed. They relied on coercion and intimidation to maintain control.

Common Roles Among Secondary Perpetrators

Handlers: Oversaw and controlled victims to ensure compliance.

Logistics Coordinators: Planned and executed larger-scale transfers or movements within the network.

Enforcers: Employed physical force, threats, or punishment to uphold order and silence.

Tertiary Perpetrators

Co-workers
   Acquaintances
   Neighbors
   Certain family members
   Unknown individuals
   They might have appeared to be everyday people in my life, but their true function was to monitor, report, and reinforce the network's control.[4]

Roles Included:

Spotters
   Observed a victim's routines or behaviors, reporting any attempts to flee or seek help.

   Informants : Gathered personal details and relayed them to traffickers.

   Surveillance Operators : Tracked and recorded a victim's activities, alerting others to any changes or potential escape plans.[5]

Living Under Constant Watch

Despite the extensive organization and clear roles I've just described, I want to emphasize that I didn't recognize the full scope of this operation while I was living through it. My everyday reality was filled with fear, confusion, and a nonstop effort just to survive.

It was only later, as I began to heal and piece together my memories, that I realized how these various individuals and roles fit into a larger trafficking system.

I also want to acknowledge that being in the school of ministry and being immersed in God's presence and truth played a major role in my eventual breakthrough. At the time, I didn't fully understand the scope of what was happening, but that immersion in God's love began to shift my perspective. This new sense of hope and possibility threatened my traffickers. They knew that if I truly escaped, I would have the chance to heal—and in doing so, I could expose the network they fought to keep hidden.

Decision Making

What led me to leave Pensacola, Florida, wasn't because I thought I was escaping trafficking—at that point, it felt inescapable, something that followed me wherever I went. The small sense of freedom I felt was all I knew, and I didn't yet realize more was possible.

My counselor, who was part of the School of Ministry, was preparing to relocate to North Carolina. I began to consider moving there as a way to continue therapy with him, or possibly moving to Missouri to be closer to the pastoral family I had grown up with.

The Beginnings of Escape

What made me leave—right before one of my biggest football games in the 2003 playoffs—was something I'll never forget.

Here's what happened:

One particular day, I filled the gas tank in my car and was on my way to work as a waitress. That morning, I noticed a strong gas smell inside the car and couldn't figure out what was wrong. What stood out even more was how quickly the gas gauge was dropping—faster than seemed normal. I was concerned, but I still needed to make it to work.

When I walked into the restaurant, my manager handed me a green folder and said, "Your father dropped this off." As you already know, my father——lived in Texas, not Florida. And as you've learned, he was my primary perpetrator.

I opened the green folder. Inside was a photo of me and my twin sister as little girls, around the age of seven. There was a red bloodstain on the picture, along with what looked like a dirt stain. Also inside was a note asking me to contact him at a hotel—he said he wanted me to come see him.

Everything clicked in that moment: the green folder, the gas smell, the rapid drop in my gas gauge, and the blood-stained picture. The color green was a known trigger for fear in my Hulk alter. It was clear—I was being warned or hunted again.

I immediately told my workplace I had to leave and wouldn't be returning.

I drove straight to a mechanic shop. It was nearly 100 degrees outside, and the gas smell had gotten worse. The mechanic pushed my car into the garage and later told me it looked like someone had tampered with the gas line.

After that, I contacted my counselor right away and told him what had happened—and that my father had tried to lure me to a hotel. Of course, I didn't meet him. Instead, I began to pack my things.

That night, I was supposed to play in the playoffs, but I was afraid my father knew where I'd be. Instead of showing up, I left everything behind and moved quickly to North Carolina.

---

1. Polaris Project. (2017). The Typology of Modern Slavery: Defining Sex and Labor Trafficking in the United States. Retrieved from https://polarispr oject.org "Systemic trafficking" refers to organized, multi-layered networks that exploit victims through coordinated roles and infrastructures. This includes familial, institutional, and transnational systems.

2. U.S. Department of State. (2023). Trafficking in Persons Report. These roles are commonly observed in both sex and labor trafficking operations, where networks assign individuals to monitor, transport, and control victims through violence or psychological coercion.

3. Van der Kolk, B. (2014). The Body Keeps the Score.

4. National Human Trafficking Hotline (Polaris). (n.d.). Understanding Human Trafficking Networks.

5. U.S. Department of Health & Human Services, Office on Trafficking in Persons. (2020). Toolkit for Building Survivor-Informed Organizations. These roles—often carried out by individuals who appear to be part of a victim's normal environment—are commonly used in trafficking networks to maintain control and prevent escape. Spotters may observe and report daily routines, Informants collect and share personal information, and Surveillance Operators track a victim's movements. These individuals may be neighbors, acquaintances, co-workers, or others coerced or recruited to support the traffickers' system of control.

Chapter 14
Entrapped Again

I thought I had finally escaped. Leaving Florida behind and moving to North Carolina felt like a fresh start. I took a job as a waitress at a corporate Italian restaurant and hoped for peace.

But soon after I resumed counseling, the trauma I thought I'd left behind began to surface. In therapy, I started talking about the abuse, the triggers, and the scattered memories from Florida. At the time, my counselor used terms like "satanic ritual abuse," "sexual abuse," and "mind programming"—because we didn't yet have the language to recognize it for what it truly was: human trafficking.

As I tried to settle into my new life, the memories returned in fragments.

One of the most intense triggers involved my former neighbor in Florida—an ex-military man who lived next door and was deeply connected to my father. At night, he would turn on a red light, and I'd get phone calls that sent me into dissociative amnesia or fugue state. [1]

I wouldn't remember what had happened or who I had spoken to—classic signs of dissociation. My mind would shut down to protect me from the overwhelming trauma. I didn't understand it then, but once I started counseling again in North Carolina, those memories slowly began to resurface.

The Beginnings of North Carolina

I moved in with a group of ministry school students who had branched off from the Brownsville Revival School of Ministry. I believed I had found a safe space—but even here, the trafficking continued.

Through the organized systemic trafficking, my father found me again in North Carolina. I began to understand that the same methods he used in Florida—using neighbors, handlers, and controlled environments—continued, just in a new location. The same patterns and tactics followed me to North Carolina, revealing how coordinated and systemic this network was.

Yet, just as I began to heal from my experiences in Florida, a new cycle of trafficking began in North Carolina. The more I uncovered, the more I understood how deeply entangled I had been in a system designed to control me. Fear and control returned, pulling me back into the cycle I thought I had escaped.

The Corporate Restaurant

At first, working at the restaurant felt normal. I had worked at a similar corporate Italian chain in Texas and had fond memories of that time. My best friend Alice also relocated to North Carolina to continue counseling for herself. She came from the revival and had a similar background in trafficking and abuse as I did, and she was pursuing healing in her own life. Like friends sometimes do, we ended up working together as waitresses at this corporate restaurant.

I can't fully explain how we ended up at a place tied to organized trafficking. Maybe it was the influence of mind programming or my father's extensive network that led us there. Either way, I want to give you a glimpse of what happened when trafficking began again in North Carolina.

Dry Storage

One night, my friend Alice and I were working the second shift. It was close to 10 p.m., and we were cleaning tables after the night rush. As I was finishing up, the assistant manager, Mike, told me that another manager wanted to speak with me in his office. When I got there, he handed me the phone—and I heard my father's voice.

Fear instantly consumed me. I froze, overwhelmed, and suddenly felt like a child again. It was a classic trigger for my DID—a trauma response I'd lived with for years. Everything after that moment became surreal. I collapsed to the floor in a fetal position, unable to speak. My regression—when I mentally reverted to a childlike state due to trauma—must have been obvious, because my manager hung up the phone with my father. [2]

Then he told me to take off my clothes. Terrified and stuck in that child state, I obeyed. He led me down the hall to the walk-in freezer. To my horror, I found Alice already there—naked, shivering, and terrified. They must have taken her while I was in the office, showing just how planned and coordinated this setup really was.

After what felt like forever, we were led to the dry storage area. It was loud, and about ten men—some coworkers, others unknown—were gathered there. In the center of the room was a video camera set up on a tripod. One man held a gun and pointed it at us like we were nothing.

They gave orders. We had no choice. Surrounded by these men—some laughing, some drinking—we were forced to perform sexual acts on each other while they recorded it. Then, both of us were raped by several of the men.

Afterward, we were threatened with death. If we told anyone, we would be killed. They said they'd use the recording to claim we consented. It was all part of the same twisted setup, and the entrapment only deepened.

After that, I was programmed to return to the restaurant at specific times late at night. The cycle of sexual abuse continued. Sometimes I was drugged after my shift ended. Other times, I just showed up because I had been told to. The fear intensified, as did the triggers and programming.

Things escalated further when I started seeing known traffickers show up at my church. My friend Alice's life was threatened if I spoke, and so was my counselor's. The pressure to stay silent was overwhelming.

The Attic

As I continued to work there, afraid to leave, sometimes finishing up a night shift, sexual abuse and rapes continued. There was an attic area in the restaurant accessed by a ladder. Up there, a mattress lay on the floor—this is where some of the assaults took place.

Golf Course

We were taken to another town a few hours away, to a golf course. During the drive, I remember feeling drugged and out of it—disoriented and detached. I was sitting in the backseat while the driver said the gate code out loud to get us in. The property was scattered with people, and though it was hard to see in the dark, the sounds were unmistakable—laughter, slurred voices, and sex. It was a drug-fueled trafficking event where multiple people engaged in group sexual acts across the golf course.

Not long after, I encountered one of the perpetrators again—he was also a server at the restaurant. One night at work, I unknowingly angered him, and he deliberately shoved me, causing me to hit the back of my head and suffer a concussion. He later tried to downplay the incident, claiming it was an accident.

Because of the severity of the concussion, I was put on medical leave. One night, while resting at Alice's house as she vacuumed nearby, something unexpected happened. I sat up suddenly and began repeating the golf course gate code. It was like my body and mind were trying to unfreeze the memory, bringing it to the surface.

Alice, too, began showing signs of trauma resurfacing—dissociation and fear. In that moment, we knew we had to do something. We decided to reach out—to the police, our counselor, and a few church leaders.

I felt heard by the police. I spent hours at the police station sharing what had happened at the restaurant. I made the police report but it is unclear if the police were able to do anything. I can only assume they didn't have enough evidence, because no charges were filed.

From my perspective, the reality of systemic trafficking was too much for church leadership—and even my counselor—to fully grasp.

Surviving the Unseen

It felt like all my hope to heal—even through counseling—was slipping away. I had no control. I felt powerless.

The same time I was trying to heal from my childhood trauma and what had happened in Florida, I was fighting to survive active trafficking in North Carolina.

I felt completely alone in it.

My Family and Learning to Break Ties

Immediately, I cut ties with the restaurant and distanced myself from anyone that I could relate or link back to that place. But my family found another way to regain control. After breaking away from the traffickers at the restaurant, I thought I had finally gained some freedom. But not long after, my older sister found her way back into my life, using my niece, Holly, to reconnect.

At the time, my sister had left her husband, remarried a military man, and moved to South Carolina. She told me that her daughter, Holly, who was 8 years old, was struggling with her new stepfather and having difficulty at school. My sister asked if it would be okay for Holly to live with me for a while. I agreed, thinking it would give her the stability she needed.

When my niece moved in with me, she began going to school and attending church regularly. Certain church members also began to nurture and support both of us, offering advice and encouragement.

At first, I wanted to believe in the relationship again, but eventually, I realized that my sister's motivations weren't entirely clear. They now seem to have been influenced by my father—another method to re-establish control.

I wanted to help my niece, but I also knew that for my healing, I had to break all family ties. Remaining in contact with those connected to my abuse—no matter how distant—kept the trauma alive. Healing required distance, clarity, and safety. Eventually, my sister came to take her daughter back, and I knew then that I had to let go—for both our sakes. It was incredibly hard, but necessary. [3]

The patterns of control were always the same. Despite my repeated attempts to escape—from Texas to Florida, and then to North Carolina—I found myself trapped in the same cycle: fear, control, and manipulation, often coming from family members and others tied to the trafficking network. Each time I thought I was free, another attempt to regain control would emerge—sometimes even through false missing persons reports.

Missing Persons Report

Even after severing all contact, my father tried one last manipulation. One Wednesday night, I skipped church service. That night, I received a call from a church leader informing me that detectives had shown up, claiming I was a missing person. The church leader and I agreed to meet with the detective the next day.

When I met with the detective, I explained that I wasn't a missing person and didn't want to be found. I knew this was just another one of my father's fear tactics—a way to keep me trapped. He had done this before, using missing persons reports as a way to exert control.

I knew I had to leave North Carolina, but I felt stuck, unsure of where to go next. The weight of uncertainty pressed on me. But deep down, I longed for what I had heard the Lord say to me when I was only five years old: "Stand up in My name, and one day, you will understand."

Hope Restored

Despite everything, as I waited and tried to figure out my next move, I turned to the only place that had ever given me peace—God. I poured out my fears in prayer, desperate for direction. I sought as much safety as I could find through church, ministry, and trying to keep a distance from anyone that I did not already know—but still not certain if I was meant to escape.

I felt my heart like a wick, almost snuffed out, but God continued to blow His love upon it, fanning the flame.

> "A bruised reed He will not break, and a smoldering wick He will not snuff out, till He has brought justice through to victory." (Matthew 12:20, NIV).

That morning, I woke up with something I hadn't felt in a long time—clarity. God had spoken to me through a dream, showing me land and a lake.

That night, our ministry team couldn't go out into the streets due to the rain. Instead, we gathered inside the church to pray. Two of the team members began to talk about a revival called the "Lakeland Outpouring."

In that prayer room, something stirred in my heart. I couldn't stop thinking about my dream. We were all desperate for more of God, and that night, at 1 a.m., we drove to Lakeland, Florida.

1. Dissociative amnesia and fugue states are dissociative responses in which a person may lose memory of significant events or personal identity, often triggered by trauma. Ross, C. A. (2007). The Trauma Model: A Solution to the Problem of Comorbidity in Psychiatry. Manitou Communications.

2. Childlike regression is a trauma response in which a person reverts to a younger mental or emotional state, often seen in survivors of prolonged or severe abuse. See: Ross, C. A. (2007). The Trauma Model: A Solution to the Problem of Comorbidity in Psychiatry. Manitou Communications.

3. Survivors of complex trauma often need to establish firm boundaries—or go no-contact—with family members involved in or complicit with abuse. This allows for the removal of ongoing emotional triggers and supports psychological recovery. See: Herman, J. L. (1992). Trauma and Recovery. Basic Books; Courtois, C. A., & Ford, J. D. (2013). Treatment of Complex Trauma: A Sequenced, Relationship-Based Approach. Guilford Press.

Part 4
Healing & Restoration

Revival Fire Press

Chapter 15
A Desperate Need for Revival

I desperately needed revival again. After everything I'd endured from trafficking in North Carolina, I felt like I was barely holding on. The trauma had worn me down. Though I tried hard to believe God still had a purpose for me, deep inside, I struggled to believe I'd ever truly be free.

Lakeland Outpouring

When I stepped into the Lakeland Outpouring revival, something shifted inside me.

The only time I had ever felt that kind of freedom was during revival. Maybe that's why I craved it so deeply—because back then, the fire of revival had begun to break chains in my life. I was hungry for God's presence. I was desperate for His healing. His presence was the only place I had ever tasted safety, freedom, and hope—and my heart ached to return to that place.

It was a hunger I hadn't felt since the Brownsville Revival—a deep longing mixed with renewed hope.

For the first time in years, I felt the calling of God on my life begin to stir again—slowly awakening.

While attending the revival, I made one mistake: I reached out to my biological mother. I hoped that even though I would only be at the revival for a short time, she might come—or at least watch it on television. I genuinely wanted her to experience God's truth, even if just through a broadcast. But reaching out to her crossed a crucial boundary. It was risky. It left me vulnerable. She didn't come—and that was the last time I ever spoke to her.

A New Beginning

After returning to North Carolina, within just a few weeks, I found myself packing my belongings and preparing to move to Lakeland, Florida. I was hoping desperately for a fresh start, but the fear of being found again remained with me. Some close friends encouraged me to change my name—something I seriously considered but hadn't yet completed. At that point, only a few trusted friends and my pastor in North Carolina knew I was moving to Florida.

After moving to Lakeland, I started taking college classes to pursue a degree in counseling—clinical mental health counseling. My own journey through trauma, and the support I received from a counselor, stirred a deep desire in me to help others heal too. Still, I wrestled with the belief that I wasn't good enough for ministry. For a long time, I thought I had missed God's original call to travel the nations and serve on the mission field. But God began to show me there was no such thing as Plan B—I had been living in Plan A all along; I just didn't know it yet. I often compared myself to ministry students who were already serving—whether in churches or overseas—and felt like I had somehow fallen behind. I battled comparison and insecurity, wondering if I had failed God. But now I can see that every moment of counseling and care I received was part of His purpose—preparing me to bring hope and healing to others coming out of the same darkness I had once known.

Meeting Terry

Soon after settling in Lakeland, I got involved with the revival church and began meeting new people. One day, while sitting with a few friends at church, I stood up to head to the bathroom when a man caught my eye. Something about him instantly intrigued me. A few days later, friends—who had no idea I'd noticed him—invited both me and this man, Terry, to dinner. As we climbed into the car, Terry joked, "If you were a bit older, I'd ask you out." Without hesitation, I said, "I don't mind." Despite our sixteen-year age difference, we quickly discovered we had a lot in common. We were both twins (though I was no longer in contact with mine), loved fishing, adored Jesus, and had a deep affection for dogs. What started as a friendship in 2008 slowly grew into a deeper relationship that eventually led to marriage later in my story. Early in our relationship, we picked out a Labrador together—Luke. I instantly fell in love with him. Luke was a gift in my life for fifteen years, offering me the kind of unconditional love my heart had longed for.

Inner Healing in Lakeland

During my time in Lakeland, I was introduced to an inner healing and deliverance ministry at the revival church. They were familiar with the type of complex trauma I had endured, including the effects of Satanic ritual abuse and human trafficking. Through their care, I began breaking free from deeply rooted lies, paralyzing fear, and layers of mind programming that had held me captive for years.

For about a year and a half, I remained in that safe space—healing, learning to trust, and slowly building relationships with those who ministered to me. As I gained strength and clarity, I revisited the idea of legally changing my birth name. By 2010, I decided to move forward, believing it could serve as a protective step toward a new beginning. I went to the courthouse and made it official. At first, it felt awkward—I didn't know how to explain it to people who had only ever known me as "Tina." But I chose the name "Davi" as a declaration of freedom and a way to reclaim the identity that had always been mine but had been buried under years of pain.

Reflection

Looking back, I believe the inner healing and deliverance team at the church played a bigger role in my safety than I realized at the time. Their understanding of human trafficking, Satanic ritual abuse, and mind control gave them insight into the kind of support I needed—spiritually, emotionally, and practically. They didn't just pray for me; they helped me recognize danger, break toxic ties, and rebuild a sense of safety in my own body and spirit. In many ways, their wisdom and discernment helped prepare me for what was coming. I truly believe they were part of God's provision to keep me safe when threats resurfaced.

Closure and Compassion

I still struggled with breaking all connections with my biological siblings. Deep down, I longed for some kind of relationship with them. Every now and then, I would search online—hoping to find a trace, a clue, anything. During one of those searches, I discovered that my biological mother had passed away a few months earlier.

Even though she had trafficked me, I still felt a deep love and compassion for her—an ache that came from that natural longing every child has for a mother. I needed closure. My soon-to-be husband, Terry, and two close friends drove with me to West Palm Beach to visit her gravesite and make sure I was safe. My heart was heavy. I never got to know the real woman God had created her to be.

When we arrived, I saw that she had no proper tombstone. Her old home was worn down, almost abandoned-looking. Seeing it all in that condition filled me with a deep sorrow for the hard life she must have lived. Moved by compassion, I decided to purchase a tombstone for her and had Psalm 139 (NIV) engraved on it—a way of acknowledging God's love over her life and allowing myself to grieve, to release, and to finally close that chapter.

A Missing Person's Report Again

By this time, I had been living in Lakeland for a solid two years, and my name had been legally changed. I was continuing to heal—reconnecting with the pastoral family I had once lived with, visiting them often for holidays like Christmas and Thanksgiving. I had made new friends, was still dating Terry, taking college classes, and faithfully attending church services.

Then, out of nowhere, I was reported as a missing person.

It started with an alarming phone call from my apartment complex manager. She told me someone claiming to be a detective from North Carolina had called and asked if I had ever lived there—using my old legal name. Thankfully, because she knew a little of my story, she didn't disclose any information. My legal name had already been changed, and that protected me in ways I hadn't even realized until that moment.

I quickly reached out to a few church leaders and contacted the pastoral family in Missouri. Together, we agreed that it was no longer safe for me to remain in Lakeland. That same day, I packed a few bags, took Luke with me, and left for Missouri. Terry stayed behind to pack up my apartment and move my belongings into storage.

Chapter 16
Healing & Restoration

I packed up my belongings into my car—whatever I could fit—and, of course, my loving Labrador, Luke, came along for the journey. Once again, I set out on a road trip to Missouri to live temporarily with the pastoral family. I hadn't lived with them since I was a teenager, and this time felt different. As I spent more time with them, I grew closer and closer to the family once again.

At that time, I was still officially listed as a missing person. When I arrived in Missouri, one of the first things I did was go to the police station to let them know I was safe. I made it clear that I did not want to be found or contacted by anyone from my past.

The family had always known me by birth name, Tabitha, but I had become insistent about being called by my new legal name, "Davie." At first, it felt awkward for them—they weren't used to it, and I understood that it would take some adjustment. But for me, taking on a new name meant everything. It was a fresh start, a way to leave the past behind and step into the life God was rebuilding in me.

Adoption and Belonging

As I stayed with them, the family continued to treat me like their daughter—just as they always had. But this time, they wanted to make it official. They asked if they could legally adopt me as an adult since I was already of age.

A lawyer helped us navigate the adult adoption process, and I stayed with them for several months while it was finalized. During that time, I became even more immersed in family life—going on vacation trips to Idaho, spending time in prayer at the International House of Prayer, and experiencing something I hadn't felt in a long time: a sense of belonging.

A New Beginning on Good Friday

In 2011, on Good Friday before Easter, we went to court for the adoption. For me and my family, the timing was prophetic—Good Friday was the day Jesus declared, "It is finished" (John 19:30). And for us, it marked the declaration that trafficking was no more. My past was put to rest, and I was given a new name and a new identity. I was legally adopted, and my last name became theirs: Virgin.

This time, my birth certificate changed, and all legal ties to my biological parents were completely severed. I no longer saw myself through the lens of what I had endured, but through the lens of who I had become in Christ. I was a Virgin—not just in name, but in spirit and identity.

Finding Love and Building a New Life

Once it became safe for me to return to Lakeland, I went back. My relationship with Terry continued to grow stronger, and eventually, he asked my adopted family for my hand in marriage. In 2012, we were married and began building our life together, moving out of Lakeland to begin the next chapter.

The early years of our marriage weren't easy for me. I struggled with anxiety, and to cope emotionally, my reliance on medication became a physical dependence that wasn't helping me heal. [1] Both my husband and my adopted parents lovingly encouraged me to seek help. I entered Teen Challenge, not far from my adopted family in Missouri, where I found a safe place to face my struggles head-on.

Healing Through Testimony

It was during my time at Teen Challenge that I began to share my testimony of being trafficked. For the first time, I learned how to speak openly about what I had endured. As I told my story to others, healing began to take root in my heart. The very act of putting my experience into words became part of my recovery.

Eventually, I became a leader in the program and began taking other students to churches where we could share our testimonies. There was something powerful about standing in front of others and declaring what God had brought me through. Each time I spoke, it felt like another layer of shame, fear, or silence was lifted off of me. I was no longer just surviving—I was stepping into healing, voice by voice, story by story.

A New Purpose

After completing the Teen Challenge program, I returned home to my husband and resumed my college degree. I began working with children and adolescents as I moved toward becoming a Licensed Professional Counselor. Reflecting on my journey, I can now see how God used my career not only to help others, but also as a continued pathway for my own healing and growth.

Once I stopped using medications and began to feel again, something deep inside me started to shift. The pain I had spent years trying to numb finally had space to rise—and as painful as it was, that's where real healing began. I wasn't just learning to help others; I was learning how to sit with my own grief, my own memories, and allow God to meet me there.

Every time I sat with a client or shared my story, I witnessed how God could turn pain into purpose.

Through counseling, I had the opportunity to offer the same hope, compassion, and support that I once needed so desperately. I began to realize that every part of my story—every heartbreak, breakthrough, and victory—had equipped me to walk alongside others through their darkest seasons. My healing was no longer just for me; it was now part of how I would help others find theirs.

God has gently led me, season after season, back to the very places where I once knew only pain. Yet this time, instead of fear, I'm walking in the beauty of His restoration. The spirit of fear no longer holds my attention. Now, it is the fear of the Lord that centers me—because the fear of the Lord is the beginning of wisdom (Proverbs 9:10). After living so long afraid of being found, retraumatized, or silenced, I've come to understand that true wisdom starts not in anxiety, but in reverent surrender. This kind of fear doesn't paralyze me—it anchors me in truth. It guards me, humbles me, and strengthens me to walk in boldness and discernment.

My faith has grown deeper. I am hungry, desperate, and thirsty to see a true move of God—not just in churches, but in hearts, homes, and entire communities

God is calling me to share my testimony boldly, to raise awareness about human trafficking, and to help prepare the Church for what's coming. I believe we are on the verge of a great awakening—and when it comes, it will carry healing for those who have lived in bondage. I want to be ready. I want the Church to be ready—to welcome the broken, the trafficked, the weary, and the wounded with truth and grace.

This calling is not about me. It's about giving all glory, honor, and praise to Jesus Christ, my Lord and savior who rescued me, renamed me, and made me whole. What the enemy used to destroy me, God has turned into a testimony of redemption. I no longer live in fear—I live in faith. I am no longer voiceless—I am a voice for the voiceless. And I will keep telling the truth, preparing the Church, and standing in the gap for the captives until every chain breaks and healing floods in like revival.

---

1. It's common for trauma survivors to develop a dependence on medication as a way of coping with emotional pain. While medication can provide short-term relief, deep healing often begins when survivors are able to feel and process emotions in safe, supportive environments (Van der Kolk, 2014). Long-term recovery involves not only symptom management, but restoring connection with the body, emotions, and others.

Chapter 17
For Such a Time As This

N ever again. Since my adoption by a pastoral family, I have not been trafficked. There is a powerful authority and covering that I believe came through that adoption—being brought into a loving, Christ-centered home where spiritual protection and identity were restored.

In many ways, my adopted family became a prophetic picture of what the Church is meant to be. They stepped in with compassion, spiritual authority, and commitment—rescuing me in ways that reflected the very heart of Jesus. Their willingness to adopt me didn't just change my life—it demonstrated what happens when the Church embraces its calling to be a refuge for the broken. It was as if God was showing me, through their actions, how the Body of Christ can rescue, protect, and restore survivors when it rises up with love and boldness.

The Church carries that same kind of authority: to stand against darkness and bring freedom to those held captive. I truly believe that when the Church steps into its God-given role as a safe haven and spiritual covering, chains break, and lives are restored.

Raising Up Survivors as Leaders

I'm not just sharing my story to shed light on trafficking—I'm here to raise up other survivors to become leaders. There is a powerful voice inside every survivor, a testimony that can break chains, stir hope, and ignite transformation. It's time we stop viewing survivors only as recipients of healing and begin empowering them to become agents of healing.

The Bible declares:

> "And they overcame him by the blood of the Lamb and by the word of their testimony..." —Revelation 12:11 (NKJV)

There is power in testimony. When a survivor stands up and shares how God met them in their brokenness, darkness trembles. Healing flows. Shame loses its grip.

I want to see a movement where survivors are no longer silent. Where they are equipped and supported to lead, to advocate, to speak boldly—not as victims, but as victors. I long for the Church to become a place that trains and empowers survivors to walk in their God-given callings, using their voices as weapons of freedom.

Healing Through Love and Acceptance

Survivors don't just need rescue—they need relationship. Real healing begins when someone looks into the eyes of a survivor and says, "You are seen. You are safe. You are loved."

The trauma survivors carry is often layered with shame, guilt, and deep-rooted feelings of unworthiness. That's why the Church must be more than a place of good sermons—it must become a refuge. A family. A place where survivors are not just tolerated, but celebrated for their courage to keep living, breathing, healing, and hoping.

Healing happens in safe spaces. That means the Church must intentionally cultivate environments where survivors feel embraced—not as fragile projects, but as powerful individuals with a purpose. It means involving them in worship, leadership, ministry, and community life—not after they've "healed enough," but as part of their healing.

Love is not passive. It leans in. It sees past the scars. It walks the long road of restoration.

If we want to see revival, we must prepare to welcome the hurting. And if we want to welcome the hurting, we must learn to love deeply and without condition.

Building a Supportive Community

If the Church is to be a place of healing, we must become intentional in how we support survivors—spiritually, emotionally, and practically. That means going beyond prayer meetings and altar calls. It means engaging in action that reflects God's heart for justice and restoration.

Here are just a few ways the Church can rise up:

Prayer and Intercession: Stand in the gap for victims and survivors. Pray against the powers of darkness sustaining trafficking networks. Pray for freedom, protection, and healing.

Raise Awareness: Teach your congregation what trafficking really looks like—how to recognize the signs and respond with wisdom and compassion.

Support Survivors: Partner with local and national organizations that provide counseling, housing, job training, and long-term care.

Advocacy: Speak out. Use your voice to push for stronger laws and more comprehensive support systems for survivors.

James 1:27 (NIV) reminds us:

"Religion that God our Father accepts as pure and faultless is this: to look after orphans and widows in their distress..."

In many ways, trafficking victims are today's orphans—displaced, overlooked, and often forgotten. The Church has a responsibility to protect, nurture, and walk with them toward healing.

A Message of Hope

Since my adoption by a pastoral family, I have not been trafficked. That truth speaks volumes about the power of spiritual covering, community, and belonging. I know firsthand what it feels like to be welcomed into a family of faith—to experience love that heals, protects, and restores.

Now the fear is no longer. The spirit of fear doesn't hold my attention anymore. Instead, I walk in the fear of the Lord, which is the beginning of wisdom

(Proverbs 9:10). My faith is stronger. I am desperate and hungry to see a move of God—not only in my life but across this generation. I long to see the Church rise up as a place of healing, ready for revival, prepared to welcome those who have been bound and broken.

Together, we can bring change. The Church can be a powerful force for healing, but it must be willing to enter the uncomfortable places—where real transformation happens. I believe God is calling His people to rise up, confront the darkness, and become sanctuaries for the hurting.

Through love, awareness, action, and the testimony of those who have overcome, we can build a world where survivors don't just survive—but thrive. Let us humble ourselves, seek His face, and pray for healing to flood our land.

Because only through Him... can we truly overcome.

Chapter 18
Revival: A Key To Freedom

Revival was never just a church service—it was God's personal rescue mission. Even when I couldn't fully grasp it, I felt the Holy Spirit moving. I watched people pour out their hearts in worship—completely lost in God's presence, singing with abandon and declaring His goodness. In my deepest despair, it felt as though God was reaching out to me—whispering that His love was real, that He had not forgotten me, and that my story was not over. Each moment in His presence became a divine appointment—God reaching out to restore my innocence and draw me back to my first love.

Looking back, I first encountered Jesus when I was just five years old, in the midst of confusion and chaos. In that tender moment, I heard His voice speak directly to my heart: "Stand up in My name, no matter what, and one day you will understand."

At the time, I didn't know what those words meant, but they settled deep into my spirit like a seed of hope. Now I see that Jesus was planting resilience and faith in me—preparing me for the battles that lay ahead.

That early encounter wasn't just a memory—it was the beginning of a divine calling, a reminder that I was never alone, even in the darkest moments.

That simple, powerful message—"Stand up in My name"—became my anchor. I began to understand that standing up in His name didn't mean the pain would instantly disappear or that I would be free from struggles. Instead, it meant that despite the brokenness, despite the fear and trauma, I would hold onto faith and trust that God was with me every step of the way.

God's love was pursuing me, reminding me that He had spoken purpose over my life long before I even knew what that meant. Every revival moment I experienced was not just emotional—it was a divine rescue. A glimpse of freedom. A taste of what healing could look like. In those atmospheres, I could sense God breathing life into places I thought were dead. They became lifelines—moments of clarity and hope that sustained me.

Revival became the hand of God reaching down from heaven, touching me, healing me, and breathing life into the broken places.

Revival is the key to freedom. And Jesus—Jesus is the key to revival.

A Revival of God's Love

Revival is not just about feeling God's presence in a worship service—it's about encountering the transformative love of Jesus. It's a love that heals, restores, and breathes life into what once felt dead and broken.

Revival must be rooted in love—the kind of love that reaches into the darkest places and declares freedom, healing, and restoration. It's not just about powerful sermons or emotional worship; it's about lives being transformed by the unconditional love of Christ. It's about creating a safe space where survivors of trafficking, abuse, and trauma can encounter God's healing touch.

What Is Love?

As I continued to journey through healing and restoration, I wrestled with one fundamental question: What is love? I saw how so many people around me seemed to struggle with love—both giving it and receiving it. I couldn't help but wonder, How can people give love if they have never truly experienced it?

As I pondered this question, I felt the Holy Spirit minister to my heart, revealing that love first comes from God. The world often tries to define love in terms of feelings, emotions, or romantic gestures, but true love is much deeper and far more powerful.

Love Demonstrated Through Jesus

"But God demonstrates his own love for us in this: While we were still sinners, Christ died for us."
—Romans 5:8 (NIV)

Jesus' sacrifice on the cross is the ultimate expression of God's love. It wasn't dependent on our merit or goodness. Instead, His love is unconditional, sacrificial, and enduring. Through this act, God reconciled us to Himself and gave us the perfect model of love to follow.

"We love because He first loved us."
—1 John 4:19 (NIV)

This is the essence of the Gospel: experiencing God's love transforms us and equips us to share it. When we encounter the depth of God's love, we are changed from the inside out. It compels us to love others with the same grace and compassion that He has shown us.

A Call for Revival

The church must become a place where God's love is not only preached but demonstrated. Revival is not just about emotional experiences or powerful sermons—it's about lives being transformed by the unconditional love of Christ. It's about creating a safe space where survivors can encounter God's healing touch.

If the church is to truly be a place of healing, it must first experience a revival of God's love—one that compels us to open our doors, embrace the broken, and walk alongside them in their journey to freedom. We need to be a people hungry for God—hungry for His presence to flood our lives, our families, our communities, and our churches.

Love That Changes Everything

Love is not just a word or feeling. Love is a person. Love is Jesus. His love pursued me through every heartbreak and moment of despair. He never let go. And now, I understand what it means to stand up in His name—redeemed, victorious, and wrapped in His relentless love.

"Love never fails."

—1 Corinthians 13:8 (NIV)

THANK YOU FOR READING

'Born into Trafficking, Rescued a Virgin'
   You've just read a true story of survival, faith—and freedom.
   But this isn't just a story—it's a movement.

JOIN THE MISSION. STAND FOR JUSTICE.

THE CALL TO STAND

A nonprofit organization mobilizing the Church & community to end human trafficking

Book a speaker
   Access trauma-informed resources
   Support survivor-led advocacy
   Take action in your school, church, or city
   www.thecalltostand.org

Acknowledgements

First and foremost, I want to thank my Lord and Savior, Jesus Christ. Without You, none of this would have been possible. You have carried me through the darkest valleys and given me hope when I thought all was lost. Your love has been my constant anchor, and Your grace has transformed my life. Thank You for never letting go of me and for giving me the strength to share my story.

To my adopted parents and my three beautiful sisters—thank you for showing me what family truly means. You opened your hearts and your home to me, offering unconditional love and support when I needed it most. You gave me the gift of safety, belonging, and acceptance. Your unwavering faith in me, and in God's power to heal, has given me the courage to keep moving forward.

To my husband—my rock and best friend—thank you for walking beside me through every step of this journey. Your kindness, patience, and understanding have been a reflection of God's love in my life. You have stood by me when the weight of my past felt overwhelming, reminding me that I am not defined by where I've been, but by the God who saved me.

To those who sat with me through my healing, who listened without judgment, offered shoulders to cry on, and created safe spaces for me to be vulnerable—I owe you more than words can express. Your presence in my pain and your support in helping me find my voice again have been invaluable.

To my faithful companion, Luke—my dog who loved me unconditionally and listened to me when I cried or just needed comfort. Your gentle presence and unwavering loyalty reminded me that love can be simple and pure. You never judged, only loved, and that meant the world to me during my hardest days.

Lastly, to every survivor who reads these pages—this story is for you. I pray that my journey brings you hope and encourages you to keep fighting. God sees you, loves you, and has a purpose for your life beyond the pain.

Thank you all from the depths of my heart. Your love and support have given me the courage to rise from the ashes and embrace the freedom Jesus promised. God bless you all.

About the author
Abigail Jordan, MA, LPC

Abigail Jordan holds a Master's degree in Counseling and is a Licensed Professional Counselor (LPC). She is a public speaker, trauma-informed clinician, and survivor of human trafficking, committed to raising awareness and advocating for revival as a key to healing and rescue for survivors across America and the nations.

As the founder of Virgin Ministries & Counseling, Abigail offers professional counseling to individuals impacted by trauma and exploitation. She also leads public speaking and educational outreach for churches, schools, and communities—equipping others to recognize, prevent, and respond to human trafficking with compassion and clarity.

With over a decade of experience in counseling and ministry, Abigail has boldly shared her testimony on the front lines—exposing the hidden realities of trafficking and declaring the healing power of God's presence. Through partnerships with churches and organizations nationwide, she brings truth to light and hope to those who need to know they are not alone.

Abigail lives in the United States with her husband of 15 years, Terry—her best friend and greatest encourager. They enjoy a peaceful life with their Labrador, Blue.

To book Abigail for speaking engagements, access survivor resources, or learn more about her work, visit: thecalltostand.org